What
Professional Virtual Assistants are Saying
About
The Commonsense Virtual Assistant

"Your book will be a great asset to many new VAs."
—*Janine Gregor, Your Virtual Wizard*

"Good luck with your book. I hope it will emphasize the importance of self-worth and encourage future VAs to value their skills, to always continue their education, and to be responsible and conscientious business owners."
—*Jennifer Dillon, Collaborative Connections*

"Sue and Joel, I really appreciate your efforts in putting this information together and look forward to the final product."
—*Margie Gibson, MG Virtual Office Solutions*

The

Commonsense

Virtual

Assistant

The Commonsense Virtual Assistant

Becoming an Entrepreneur
Not an Employee

by
Joel D Canfield
and
Sue L Canfield

Illustrations by
Joel D Canfield

Published by BizBá6
Copyright 2009 Joel D and Sue L Canfield

BizBa6
Joel D Canfield
286 Alta Vista Avenue
Roseville CA 95678

Who knows; if you ask nicely, we might send you a free copy of the digital version of this book.
ISBN 978-0-9840940-1-1

To my Best Beloved

A Note from Sue

My work experience began at the age of 17 as an assistant in an insurance office. After 24 years working for other people, I started my own business in 2005 as a virtual office professional. This last year I met many virtual assistants online who asked me about my business and how they can succeed as virtual assistants. The more I communicated with other virtual assistants, the more I realized that new and aspiring VAs (Virtual Assistants) needed basic guidance on how to run a business.

Since Joel and I have owned and operated our own businesses for many years, we wanted to share some basic commonsense information that can help you as a new or aspiring VA run a successful business. This information will also help those looking for a dependable virtual assistant know what they should expect from a virtual assistant.

There are many more things that could be covered in more detail. Maybe we'll put them in the next book.

Thank you to the many virtual assistants from across the country who replied to my requests for comments on what it takes to succeed as a virtual assistant. Some of your comments are included throughout the book.

And One from Joel

Sue and I have worked together for years. We wouldn't change it for the world. This book will help you see how you can be just as happy working for yourself as we are.

I consider all business challenges, human challenges, with a human solution. Business today is broken, and the solution is to become more human, not more technical or more money-oriented.

There are a lot of 'how to' guides out there. This is not one of them. This is more of a 'why to' guide, to help you see how people think, and how you should think, to get genuine satisfaction from your business.

When it comes to the skills we use (or would like to use) to make a living, many of us are self-taught. Often this leaves holes in our education. Some we're aware of, others, we're not. This book will help ferret out the latter and allow them to be filled in before they cause problems.

The 'commonsense' part of the title refers to the fact that little, if any, of this information is revolutionary in nature. Its purpose is to help you ensure that your foundation is solid and complete.

Introduction

So You Want to Be a Virtual Assistant

The virtual assistant industry is growing rapidly. Just about anyone can *say* they are a virtual assistant. You have a computer, internet access, and the desire to work from home. Voila! You're a virtual assistant.

But is that enough to succeed as a virtual assistant? Do you have what it takes to run a business?

Yes, a virtual assistant is a business owner. Successful business owners need to have good business sense. As a business owner, you, the virtual assistant, need to understand what it takes to run a business.

Running a successful business entails a variety of tasks. Just some of the things you want to consider when running a business as a virtual assistant are:

- Business plans and mission statements
- How to read and understand profit and loss statements

- Set rates and revenue goals
- Do you need to hire a business coach, tax accountant or attorney?
- Create action plans and branding strategies
- Follow a code of ethics
- Business licensing
- Contracts
- Insurance
- Client file structure
- Project tracking
- Time management

Skills & Tools You'll Need

Of course, you'll need the actual administrative skills clients will expect from a virtual assistant (or any assistant, for that matter.) While this book isn't about those skills, we're including a short and certainly incomplete list of things we'd consider essential for any VA.

- Excellent spelling, punctuation and grammar. Not just good. If you're not exceptional, you'll struggle.
- A professionally designed website. Joel does web development for a living. He knows that, while your neighbor's nephew or niece can build your website, they aren't necessarily going to create the most search-engine and user friendly, easily-maintained professional presence for you.
- A place to work undisturbed when necessary. Your clients do not want to picture you working in your jammies at home, even if they know that's what you're doing.

- A reliable computer not shared by other family members. You don't want your significant other or the kids wreaking havoc, even accidentally, with your clients' files and your hard work.
- Reliable internet access. Otherwise, you're not virtual.
- A reliable printer. Color laser printers are inexpensive enough that, if you're buying something new, that's a good option. Another option would be an all-in-one device: printer, scanner, fax and copier.
- Reliable phone service—preferably with cheap long distance. You'll be on the phone a lot. You don't want to spend a fortune on long distance, and you don't want to be worried about the cost if your client needs time to chat.
- Dependable transportation—virtual sometimes includes driving to the post office, the office supply store, and whatnot.
- Basic knowledge of email
- Word processing software—preferably Microsoft Word; whether or not it's the best, it is the industry standard.
- Spreadsheet software—again, Microsoft's Excel is what most folks use.
- Time-tracking ability—your accounting software, Excel, something more than notes on a scrap of paper.
- Reliable local print shop—printing is a professional job; don't assume you can fill your clients' print needs unless that's your profession.
- Business cards
- Letterhead—you're a professional; look like one.
- Know how to create a business letter
- A tool to create PDFs (Adobe's portable document format)—there are free tools at Adobe's site (http://www.adobe.com/acom/createpdf) for one-off needs, and inexpensive tools like PDF995

(`http://pdf995.com`) which are adequate. You probably don't need the expensive Adobe Acrobat software. The Adobe Reader, which is free, allows you to view PDFs, but not create them.

- A business checking account. This is separate from your personal checking account. That's why they're named the way the are.
- Accounting software for invoicing—whether you use an online service or software on your computer, tracking your own income and expenses and creating client invoices can get very complicated if you don't have the right tool to manage the process.
- Meet any legal requirements for operating a business where you live. Will you need a business license? Will you need a license to operate a business from your home? Do you need to file a fictitious business name statement? Find out what the requirements are where you live. Some places, they're minimal. Other places, you can be in serious trouble if you don't cross all the Ts and dot all the Is.

Optional and Advanced

These tools and services are nice to have; many are free. We use them all.

- PayPal account—Once upon a time PayPal (`https://www.paypal.com`) was the unwanted step-child of the credit card world. These days, most folks don't think twice about using it. We receive just as many payments via PayPal as we do by check.
- A toll-free phone number—It's cheap. You can get a toll-free number for about $10/month most places.

Ours includes enough minutes that we rarely pay anything additional. Don't make your clients pay for phone calls. (Another fun thing: most phone companies are willing to spend some time helping you find a 'vanity' number, one that spells something. We just recently got the toll-free number 877.3 BIZBA6— prefix, a single number, and our business name. Pretty cool.)

- Online file transfer—Fast internet access is becoming the norm. Rather than waiting for a CD in the mail, transfer even very large files online. Box.net (http://box.net) has a free version, and inexpensive paid versions. If you have a friendly helpful webmaster, they can set up something similar which would have little or no ongoing cost.

- Internet phone—Skype (http://www.skype.com) allows you to use your computer or a regular phone to make phone calls over the internet instead of a regular phone service. A single monthly fee for all your calls, local, long distance, or international. GoogleTalk (http://www.google.com/talk/) is free, and allows you to use your computer's microphone and speakers or a headset to talk to other GoogleTalk users.

- Jing (http://www.jingproject.com) is a great tool for creating tutorials and demos. Start it up and do a screen and audio capture from your computer. Show a client how to do something, once, and they can watch the file and listen to your explanation as many times as they need to.

- Digital faxing—eFax (http://www.efax.com)gives you a real fax number folks can use, and you'll receive an emailed PDF of the fax. For a fee, you can use them for outgoing faxes as well. Your own fax machine is the best option, but eFax is a viable alternative.

- Digital signatures—Echo Sign (http://www.echosign.com) is an easy-to-use system which uses email and digital encryption to allow you and a client to sign documents without having to wait while paper is shuffled back and forth through the mail.

Yes, it's a lot. You may have good reasons why some of it's unnecessary. But remember that a prospect who's looking for just the right VA may assume you have the list of basics above, and might just assume you have some of the advanced stuff, too. Don't risk disappointment if you don't have to. If you have any questions or comments on this list, we'd love to discuss it—it's one reason our contact information is at the back of this book.

"For those of you looking to launch a VA practice (or any business, for that matter!), spend as much time delving into business development as you do learning technology and perfecting your service offerings."
—Rachel Rasmussen, Rescue Desk, LLC

Business Owner vs. Employee

A virtual assistant is no longer an employee. A VA is a business owner. The service we offer is virtual assistance. But our title really is Owner. In order to be taken more seriously, many virtual assistants give themselves a title that reflects the fact that we are business owners and not just 'assistants'. My title is Virtual Office Administrator. Others call themselves Internet Marketing Strategists or create a title that reflects their skill set.

The point is that a virtual assistant is a business owner. When you think of yourself as a business owner, your actions will reflect that and your clients will respect you as a business owner.

"I believe one of the things it takes to succeed as a virtual assistant is a total mindset change. After working in the corporate world for years, it is tough to get out of the employee mindset and into the business owner mindset. And not everyone is destined to be a business owner. You have to weigh the pros and cons, then determine if it's right for you. Once you have made that determination, then comes hard work and persistence."
—Vickie Turley, A Balanced Alternative

"Owning and running a business is not for the faint of heart. But with dedication, commitment, and enthusiasm it will be one of the most rewarding adventures you'll ever undertake."
—Rachel Rasmussen, Rescue Desk, LLC

Chapter One: How We Think

I'm Unique, Just Like Everyone Else

We each think we're pretty special.

Despite the fact that we're physically more or less like everyone else, despite the fact that traits like intelligence, good looks, physical ability, and virtually anything else are distributed fairly evenly amongst humankind, we *feel* unique.

Are you a good driver? Most people would say they are. Are you, say, in the top 10% of the drivers on the road?

Most people would say they are.

We can't all be in the top 10%, but somehow, one at a time, we put ourselves there.

How well do you get along with other people? You seem like a nice person, so I'm not surprised that you think you're easy to get along with. In fact, you're probably in the top half when it comes to good-natured easy-to-deal-with, right?

So is everyone else. Every man in the United States (and probably women, too, and probably the whole world) rates himself as being in the top half in popularity. When I studied math, the top half was reserved for about 50% of any sample. But we're talking about people, not math.

There's our first hint: people aren't math; people aren't statistics. People are fundamentally emotional creatures. People are categorically, absurdly positive about themselves. It's a good thing. We'll come back to it later.

We are each thoroughly convinced of our absolute uniqueness. It's obvious to us that no one else could possibly be just like us. We want our singularity to be recognized. In fact, we often demand it.

Remember the last time you had a coupon that expired yesterday? Or the special that was only good for one, but you needed two? What did you do?

Many perfectly normal sane people ask to be treated as exceptions. If you haven't done it yourself, you've heard it; the person ahead of you in the line with eleven items in the ten-items-or-less lane, paying with a check when the sign says 'Cash Only'. And you're thinking the whole time, "Why should they sneak an extra item through? If you don't have cash, don't go through the 'Cash Only' line!"

And there's the rub: you know, deep inside, that they're not special. They're like everyone else. They should play by the rules, take their turn, and not cause a fuss.

Yes, we're special.

They're not.

Certain challenges arise in a world full of people who think "I'm special; you're average." The most skillful social types have learned that you can't treat people as if you believe this. They have, in fact, learned that the most successful behaviour is to turn it around, and treat others as if they were just as unique and special as they think they are.

Relationships

So then, how do we create a really valuable relationship between two people who each think they're the center of the universe, and the other is simply an orbiting asteroid?

Ah, here's where the truth smacks us upside the head.

Because, see, you're not unique. Not really. Neither am I. Fundamentally, we all have the same needs; we all have the same wants. And the only way to truly develop a relationship, even in business, is to genuinely believe that the other party is important. In fact, more important than you.

Starting right here, I'm going to assume that you're ready to at least try to act as if every person you do business with, whether client, sub-contractor, employee, partner, or vendor, is special and unique. As with the broader scope of Carnegie's book, my philosophy on the human relations fundamental to business just isn't the same otherwise.

What Do They Want?

Let's look under the hood for a few minutes, and see if we can isolate some of the quirky attitudes most of us share. But first, let's spend a moment on why we care.

There is no Reality; Only Perception

We all see the world and the people in it through glasses of our own chosen color, rose or not. It's virtually impossible to see someone's actions objectively, to hear their words by their dictionary definitions. We each came to this point in life by our own path, and the experiences and people and knowledge along the way have shaped our thinking, our expectations, and our perception of others.

While there is certainly a reality here somewhere, no two of us experience it in the same way. (Fine, fine; we're unique. I'll find different words for when we're unique and when we're not.)

What happens, then, is we have these moments of confusion like something from a television sitcom. An innocent comment or question evokes an intense, perhaps even ferocious response. Someone else's filters are different enough from our own to take offense at what we thought was a simple question.

It takes practice, lots of it, to perceive others' filters, the preconceived notions they bring to every human transaction. In the meantime, there are ways to avoid negative reactions as much as possible, and to enhance the positive. Most of the time you can reduce the threat levels to an acceptable point by being more aware of just what it is people want.

It's Work

Look down any alley near where you live. Look out in your yard or garden. If you plant flowers, you get flowers. If you plant weeds, of course you get weeds. If you plant nothing, you get—weeds.

In the absence of positive effort, the default for dirt is to grow weeds, not to sit idle.

The same is true in our relationships. If you look for the bad in people, you'll find it. But in the absence of a positive effort to see the good, you'll see their negative traits. The only way to really see what makes this employee or customer special and unique is to actively look for it.

It takes time. It takes effort. It takes really wanting it; really believing that it's there. And it is; in all but the rarest cases, anyone who works for you, anyone who comes to you for professional help has something about them that will enhance your professional life. Find it, acknowledge it, learn from it.

They'll appreciate it. They might just return the favor.

The Most Beautiful Sound

Remember your last visit to the doctor's office, and they mispronounced your name? C'mon; it's not that hard.

Even if it's an uncommon name, they should be able to get it right by now, shouldn't they?

How would you feel if your diploma, trophy, or invitation had your name misspelled?

We consider our name the label of our uniqueness. I am not 'Joe'; never have been, never will be. And I can't tell you the dozens of mispronunciations of my last name I've heard over the years. Honest; it's two simple English-language words. But after nearly half a century, I'm still slightly miffed when someone who obviously considers English their mother tongue can't pronounce it correctly.

Names are sacred. If you remember one single fact about a person, remember their name. Know how to pronounce it. Want more extra points than you can count? When you meet someone whose name is difficult to pronounce in your language, make an effort to get it right. Even if you're not perfect, they'll appreciate the sincere effort.

A person's name pronounced correctly is, to them, the most beautiful sound in the world. Get it wrong and you may as well have sprayed graffiti on the Mona Lisa.

Emotional Bank Accounts

In any ongoing relationship, we keep track. It's not usually intentional; we just do it. Stop and think for a moment: who's that one friend you just know you owe a favor? They know it too. You know some people who always seem to be taking: they're the ones who are always late, or cancel at the last minute. They ignore the little details like forgetting your anniversary.

But you also know the folks who show up on time. They send a card on your anniversary. They don't surprise you by expecting more than you thought was agreed on; they'll borrow your lawn mower but they don't expect you to deliver it, and they return it full of gas and cleaned up a bit.

Every transaction in an ongoing relationship makes deposits to or withdrawals from another person's emotional bank account. And it's human nature for us to have at least a general idea of the other guy's balance with us, and ours with them. You have a gut feeling when you ask for a ride to the bus stop because your car won't start again that your neighbor is going to be annoyed, even if he agrees to take you. You're overdrawn.

You probably also know how it feels to have someone who's always been there for you ask a favor for themselves. If it's in your power, you do it; they've made so many deposits that a reasonable withdrawal seems trivial.

Making a genuine effort to understand people, paying attention to details, keeping your word, avoiding unpleasant surprises; they're all deposits.

Apologies can be deposits, too. Inadvertently made a withdrawal by forgetting an appointment or breaking something you borrowed? A sincere apology makes a deposit. The nature of the relationship, your current balance, has an effect on the value of the deposit, but it's a positive nonetheless.

Beware, though: repeatedly withdrawing, assuming that an apology will fix it, can bankrupt you in a flash. People know when they're being taken advantage of.

Communication Mirroring

A few years ago I was trying to complete a search tool for a client. It seemed that no matter how many emails I sent to the hosting contact, things moved like molasses, and often in the wrong direction. I'd send an email, they'd leave a voicemail on my phone, I'd email to correct their confusion, and so on. (Have I mentioned how much I used to hate talking on the phone?)

Finally, in frustration, I actually picked up the phone. Things were resolved, correctly, in less than five minutes. I don't know how much evidence I'd been given before this, but in a camel/straw moment I realized that I'd been using my style of communication instead of his. As soon as I mirrored what he'd been trying to do all along, the dam burst.

We all have our favorite method of communication. Mine is email. One friend rarely emails more than three words, but will stay on the phone as long as I'm willing to.

Just like we don't get to choose how we're perceived by others, we can't successfully shove people into our communication method. A prospect who emails should get an email, not a phone call, in return. While the email should be sent off just as quickly as you'd answer the phone (email-oriented types tend to expect email to be almost real-time) a phone call response to an email can feel pressuring and invasive.

On the other hand, if someone leaves you a voicemail, or you're following up on a phone call, use the phone; email will seem impersonal to phone-oriented communicators. Email always sounds a bit less friendly than you write it; write a friendly message and it sounds flat and direct; write something that's flat and direct, and it sounds angry and rude—especially to someone accustomed to the warmth and instantaneous reaction of a human voice.

And, yes, if someone writes you a letter, you write a letter. Even further, if they hand wrote their letter, do the same.

Be what people expect, not what you're used to being.

Persuasion

Business is about persuasion. Whether customers or employees, you're going to have to understand something about how people think to have any success.

More Carrot, Less Stick

One issue that particularly plagues big business can still be a deal-breaker for the small business. Most businesses act as if all their customers and employees were lazy, dishonest, and generally untrustworthy.

We go through life assuming that, for the most part, the folks around us aren't actually evil. (Of course, if you honestly believe that your customers and employees really are just waiting for their chance to lie, cheat, and steal, please give this book as a gift to someone you don't understand.)

Why, then, when we hire them to work for us, or encourage them to buy our products or services, do we suddenly expect them to earn our trust? Sure, there are some bad apples. I'm not foolish enough to leave cash laying around the office, for instance.

Try this: instead of making people earn our trust, make them earn distrust. I know from experience that in a trusting environment, the bad apples stick out like they had a neon arrow over their heads. Treat people like grown-ups. They'll behave like grown-ups. If not, you'll know pretty quickly.

This doesn't mean allowing anarchy. You expect certain behaviour from adults. Give them leeway, but set expectations. When you toss the time clock, make it clear that someone still has to be there to open the store or answer the phones or fire up the oven on time, or work doesn't get done. Showing up on time to start work is so much more meaningful than showing up on time to clock in.

Why Choose Lose/Lose?

Most of us see persuasion as negotiation, and see negotiation as competition, a 'zero sum game'. For me to win, you have to lose. It's not much of a step from there to 'your loss is my win.'

We've all heard about trying for a win/win situation; we could extrapolate the four combinations of win and lose. Stephen Covey's "7 Habits of Highly Effective People" teaches us a new paradigm of human interaction: win/no deal. Win/no deal is where the action is.

Of course, we all want the win/win situation. You get exactly what you wanted, I get exactly what I wanted; it's great. But what if one of us wasn't going to win? For instance, you want to hire me, but can't afford to pay what I need to earn. Under the traditional four-way paradigm, we have three choices. You could pay more than you can afford so I make what I need. From your perspective that's lose/win. I could take the job at what you're paying (win/lose.) Finally, everybody's favorite, the compromise; we split the difference.

This last one, everyone's favorite—that's lose/lose. The worst of all worlds. You're paying too much. I'm not earning enough.

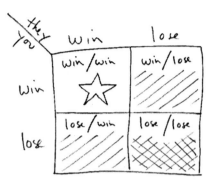

The real answer to this situation is win/no deal. We find a win/win situation, or we agree that I can't work for you. Mind you, we're not talking about greed here. We've agreed to be honest with each other. Even though neither of us is focusing on the money, finance does have to enter the picture. You really can't afford more; I really can't work for less.

No deal. I simply can't work for you. Unless we can find a way to change the situation, we choose 'no deal'. We both go away happier than if we'd chosen what has become the default setting in modern business: the lose/lose.

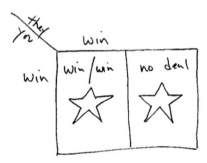

Compromise = Waste

You may have guessed that my default setting is to avoid compromise. The previous section on lose/lose is one example. Here's another. With my sincerest apologies, I'm going to bring up some math.

If you're the right age, you remember Venn diagrams from school; circles of different sizes, usually overlapping to some degree. A Venn diagram of your skills, perspectives, and feelings and mine can show the difference in value between compromise and its well-behaved sibling, synergy.

There you are, on the left, that nicely rounded circle full of talents, skills, knowledge, experiences.

Over there, on the right: that's me. In the book, at least, we're the same size. I'm filled with my own talents, skills, knowledge, experiences.

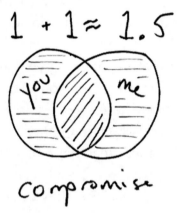

Compromise, by its nature, means that if we work together, the circles overlap. You bring what I understand and share; I bring what you understand and share. We get certain economies of scale, certain shared styles, beliefs, skills, which makes our value increase.

In this compromise, 1 + 1 might equal about 1.5.

Synergy; ah, synergy. This is where we revel in our differences.

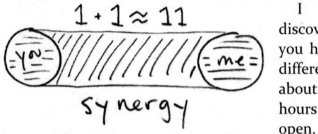

I may discover that you have totally different ideas about what hours to be open. I may have a perspective on selling via the internet that you've never considered. Compromise means we both give something up in order to work together. Synergy means we both *accept something new* in order to work together.

Accepting, even reveling in our differences, synergy means that 1 + 1 = 11, maybe more.

Find out something you didn't know about a customer, employee, vendor, partner, competitor. Figure out why they think or act that way. Figure out why you don't. Chances are, synergizing what you've learned will add much more to your quality of business life than the effort it took learning it.

If I Could Change Your Mind

Business is about persuasion. (Wait; I already said that. Well, it is.)

Here's another fundamental truth: you can not change another person's mind. Can't. Not possible. The very best hope you have is of giving them enough information so they'll change their own mind.

Oh, there's more. Carnegie's rule says "seek first to understand, then to be understood." We've all felt the wrong end of that stick.

When my children were very young (and so were those of all my friends) there was one couple who were the world's greatest experts on child-rearing. They had an answer for everything, and were so enthusiastic that you didn't even have to ask for their advice; they offered it unbidden at every opportunity.

It didn't seem to matter that they had no children of their own.

When you don't feel that someone understands your situation, how much value to you place on their advice? Not much, I'll wager. Advice, conjured out of some clinical vacuum in another person's head, carries no weight with us. But show me you understand me, and I just might listen.

I have this conversation with my middle daughter quite often (but, thankfully, less often as time goes by.) I request, suggest or recommend a certain action. She suggests that I don't know what I'm talking about. I ask for details, probe for reasons. Generally, I do my best to find out what she's thinking and why. And she knows that's what I'm doing.

Then, based on what I've gleaned, often using her own arguments, I explain why I'm still right. Unless, of course, I'm not. My oldest son learned early in life that *after* he'd said, "Sure, Dad; I'll do that" he could also say "but, what about this?" and if he was right and I was wrong, we did it his way. There's another one of those secret weapons: humility enough to admit, emphatically, when you're wrong, or maybe just not right enough. To your kids, your spouse, your employee, your customer. Remember, a sincere apology is a deposit in your emotional account with them.

No rational person enters a disagreement knowing they're wrong. Some folks discover it along the way, and have a hard time backing down, but to begin, we each think it's the other chap who's got the wrong end of the stick.

Remember, that person you're trying to persuade knows in their heart of hearts that they're brand new, special, and unique. They figure you're pretty average. The question is, do you want to win an argument, or do you want to persuade? (Tip: the only way to win an argument is to avoid it in the first place.)

As soon as you realize someone disagrees with you, whether customer, employee or partner, stop talking, and start listening. Find out why they think they're right.

Because they do; they most sincerely believe they've got the picture. Thing is, maybe they do. But your only hope of finding out, and persuading them otherwise if they're wrong, is to begin by understanding their perspective.

If after careful appraisal you're still convinced that you need to adjust their thinking, you're in a much better position to do so. You've shown the courtesy of listening. They're less likely to feel like you're talking down to them, or that you don't understand. Now, based on their own take on the situation, you can explain clearly and simply why you disagree.

There's another slant to all this (you didn't think we were done already, did you?)

Once you've got someone listening, persuasion is easy, right? All you have to do is show them logically why you're right and they're wrong, and they'll wholeheartedly support you.

We all know better. But why?

Picture two babies in the nursery. Which is cuter, yours or theirs? Unless you're not from the same planet as I am, your own baby is cuter than anyone else's; cuter, in all likelihood, than any baby since they started making 'em.

People's ideas, beliefs, even actions, are their babies. You may have the perfect method for doing this or that; you've perfected it over your 12 years in business, you've tried other ways, and you just know. Doesn't matter; that other person's idea, new and untested and unknown is their baby.

Show them that it's ugly, and you have most emphatically not made a convert.

Persuasion is a subtle art. It requires humility. You must begin from the belief that the point you're championing is, in fact, the best option for the other guy. If that's the case, it does not matter if you get credit for your brilliance. In fact, you're much better off if you can lead the conversation around, through questions and listening, to the point that this younger or less experienced one comes to your conclusion on their own.

Yup; let them think it was their idea. Now, whose baby's the cutest? Still theirs, they've just got a new baby, that's all.

You'll never change someone's mind by telling them they're wrong. You may be able to embarrass or frighten or cajole someone into doing things your way for now, but in the long run, they'll either slip back or slip away to another employer.

Decisions, Decisions

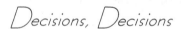

You'd think decisions would be easy. If there are two options, you'll prefer one over the other. If there are three, one will outshine the rest.

Some folks behave exactly as you'd expect: have a preference, express it, done. But often, it's not that simple.

How often have you stood in line behind someone at the coffee shop or fast food joint who just couldn't make up their mind? It's not a rare occurrence.

There are a number of reasons the average person might have trouble making a decision.

1. There are too many choices. There's a corollary: most folks will readily accept a package deal, but don't want to bother ordering a la carte.
2. They can't differentiate between options. This could be because they don't have enough information, because there really isn't enough difference, or because they're just not paying attention to the details.
3. There aren't enough choices: what they really want isn't available, or they just can't find it.

You can solve or avoid every one of these.

Too Many Choices

In the face of too many choices, many people fall back to what's popular. If your products or services contain an obviously favorite option, that's fine, if that's what you want to sell. If they don't, you have a better chance of making the sale if you make choice easier. It's very common in software design to have a plethora of options so folks can configure everything exactly the way they want.

The trouble with that is the most folks, rather than appreciating the flexibility, never change a thing. Most software is designed by people who think like computers, and it shows. The very excellent text editor I'm using right now has this option in the preferences:

☐ Display startup logo

Yes, that's exactly what it sounds like: when the program is started, should I be forced to wait an extra three seconds while the manufacturer's logo fills my screen, or would I like to just start using the program?

Who does that benefit? Imagine if you car offered to play a Buick radio ad every time you got in. Or, you could turn it off (the logo option in my text editor is on by default.)

I cannot imagine any possible benefit this could have to the customer. Not many options available in your service are likely to be this obviously self-serving, but you really ought to review any choices you're foisting off on your clientele and see which ones really add value to their buying experience.

The Meal Deal

Sometimes, a package makes sense. Too much granularity can just become a nuisance. Imagine if you had to describe the contents of your salad: which lettuces (yes, there is more than one kind of lettuce) and vegetables, what kind of croutons, dressing choices—you'd eat even fewer salads than you do now.

My web development company nearly always includes a quote for hosting and email when we bid on a website development project. We keep the numbers separate for those who don't plan to use our services for those items, but so many small business operators don't realize that those things aren't automatically included that we realized it just made sense to draw their attention to it.

Is there an add-on, option, or special service you really wish your clients would use more, something that would make the experience better for them in the long run? Add it. If it's really the right thing to include option B with service A, just make option B an integral part of service A, adjust the price if necessary, and remove one more unnecessary decision.

And when a referral comes to you and asks for service A a la carte, like their friend used to get, explain why you've include option B—and if they turn it down, give them what they want. This isn't about removing valid choices, it's about reducing unnecessary ones.

Not Enough Perceived Difference

If you have two options which really are quite similar, look at your sales figures. Ask customers and prospects why they choose one over the other. Chances are you'll find very little reason to maintain the two subtly different options.

If you've been operating for any length of time, though, you may have already weeded out the near-duplicates. At least, from your side of the window. It never ceases to amaze me, though, how little attention people pay to the fine print, technical specifications, and other information you'd think would help them see the difference between the Silver Service and the Gold Service.

Remember: there's no reality, only perception. If your prospect can't tell the difference between your Silver and your Gold, and Silver is less expensive, what rational person would choose the more expensive option?

People don't really notice details. When we see something new, the way we wrap our heads around it is to compare it to something we already know, and focus on the differences. If the differences aren't overt and obvious, we're likely to conclude this is just another of whatever we're already familiar with.

You can imagine the unhappiness all around when Planter's packaged their fresh roasted peanuts in a foil vacuum pack container which looked exactly like the packages ground coffee often came in. Whose fault was it when people gummed up the store's coffee grinder, thinking it was a new brand of coffee? You could blame the customers, of course; it was written right there on the package that it contained peanuts, not coffee.

Making your prospects and customers feel dumb is no way to do business, though. Accept that most folks don't pay much attention to the details; instead, they look for comparisons to and differences from something familiar, and ignore the rest. Make the differences obvious. Otherwise, you may find folks missing out on the added benefits of your Gold Service, which they would have chosen had they only known the details. Just as bad, you risk making someone feel dumb just after (or maybe just before) they've given you their money.

Not Enough Perceived Choices

Long before that ice cream parlour introduced the idea of 31 flavors to choose from instead of just chocolate and vanilla, folks were already used to the idea of the thousands of choices offered in mail order catalogs. Even with big items like cars, there are currently hundreds of models to choose from.

In some services, the number of options isn't as great; we're not all Starbucks, with 16.7 million ways to make a cup of whatever. And sometimes, more options exist, but we don't offer them, either by choice or necessity.

I remember something that happened in a small pharmacy in Texas. While I was waiting in line, an elderly customer asked about a particular brand of whatever she was looking for. The pharmacist shook his head and said, "We don't carry that brand, but we have this one." When the woman said she really preferred the brand she'd gotten at his competitor's store across the street, he pulled some cash out of the till and said to his assistant, "Will you please run across the street and get our customer the brand she prefers." And then refused payment.

If that had happened to me I can't imagine ever shopping anywhere else. It may not be feasible to give your customer a freebie at your competitor's place of business, but if you know the chap down the street does exactly what they need, and you don't, do the right thing for your customer. Don't create a choice where there is none. In the long run, integrity will win out over greed.

In these days of the long tail, however, sometimes it's only the perception of a lack of choice. You just might have exactly what they need, but if they can't find it, it's the same as if you didn't offer it at all.

The stories I read of excellent service carry too much of the element of astonishment to make me think that good service is expected by the average consumer. That tells us that making a prospect find someone to ask about this, that, and the other thing isn't going to work. Make it easy to figure out that you offer what they want. Whether it's big print, clearer descriptions, simpler lists, better organization, or printed maps of your store, until you have a universal reputation for excellent service among your clients and prospects, making them ask is an invitation to look elsewhere.

No One Likes Surprises

At least, not after the age of three.

I love music. I love everything about music. Not all styles (some stuff that gets recorded, put on a CD, and sold in music stores, online and off, is not music) and not everything in the styles I like. But if it's about music, there's something there for me.

I've written in the past that liner notes sell albums; good liner notes sell bands. One thing I love about Loreena McKennitt's albums is the massive and extensive liner notes; she's a musicologist who performs her research. I love Bob Dylan's whimsical musings. I like learning that Alan Parsons, of the Project, was the recording engineer on the first Wings album, and that Tony Levin played bass for the other members of Yes when Chris Squire worked on other projects, taking the band's name with him temporarily.

I learned all that from liner notes. LaLa.com doesn't care about liner notes, and they assume you don't, either.

Or, perhaps, they know you do, but don't want you to realize that they don't. Some months back, I signed up for this innovative legal way to swap CDs. I always have a few I'm looking to unload for various reasons, and thought it would be cool to send 'em off to someone who wanted Gretchen Wilson's CD, and in a very 'pay it forward' manner, get in return, from an entirely different member of the group, Eric Clapton's "Me and Mr. Johnson."

Until it arrived.

Sans case, liner notes, anything. Just the bare CD in the plastic case with LaLa's logo stuck on it.

After emailing the sender and LaLa's support team, I finally found the obscure hidden reference to the fact that they encouraged members to ship only the bare CD, since it would save costs; otherwise, you'd have to stick on extra postage beyond what LaLa provided.

How could they be smart enough to provide postage up front, and so dumb they hid information that was potentially critical to their prospective members? Their response to me was that I could wait a while until their 'deluxe' (read 'more expensive') version was ready. My response was that if they hid one deal-breaker from me, and didn't seem to care when I stumbled across it, what else weren't they telling me?

Trust lost.

The sad thing is that they could have had it both ways. For years I've been buying CDs online from New World Records (NewWorldCDs.com) and they offer what owner Terry Allan calls 'flat shipping.' Instead of the heavy, expensive-to-ship jewel case, they ship the CD in a vinyl sleeve. It's designed to hold the cover booklet on one side, and the tray insert and CD on the other. The entire package fits, and it's even lighter than the clamshell cases LaLa used.

I checked again recently, and don't see any mention of the 'ship you the whole CD package' version. Or of CD trading at all. And, I had to create an account to find out anything about how it works now.

The lesson learned is this: it's much, much better to make a potentially negative aspect obvious, right up front, than to let your suspects/prospects discover it on their own. Of course, the better lesson is not to introduce the potentially negative aspect in the first place. Sure, that takes creativity, effort, and wanting it. Welcome to entrepreneurship, using what I like to call 'the right way.'

It is very important that a virtual assistant communicates clearly with their clients so each party knows what to expect. Be clear about how many hours you expect a project to take and keep your client informed. If it appears that a project will take longer than expected, let your client know as soon as possible. Never surprise your client by going over the agreed hours and then presenting a bill for those extra hours.

Do not agree to take on a project for which you don't have the skill set, unless you have someone you know you can sub-contract the work to that does have the skills. If you agree to take on a project but don't have the abilities needed to accomplish it, you will harm your reputation and lose a client. It's much better to be upfront with the client and explain that you don't have those skills and offer to help them find someone who does. The client will appreciate your honesty and be much more likely to use your services for projects you are able to handle.

We were recently contacted by a prospect that needed skills we didn't specialize in. We contacted another virtual assistant and connect the two of them. The prospect appreciated our honesty and willingness to connect him with someone who had the necessary skills. We discussed the types of tasks we would be able to help him with and we look forward to working with him on a future project. As a nice bonus, the VA we referred to this prospect has since referred another client to us and we're now working together.

Once you begin working with a client and it becomes apparent they need skills beyond what you have, let them know and make arrangements for someone else to handle those tasks. Don't try to do what you don't do. In the end, you'll disappoint your client and damage your reputation for excellence.

Chapter Two: Personal Habits

Manners Matter

Not just socially; we all know manners matter socially.

Manners matter in business. Good social skills, in fact, are critical to the success of any business.

Let's talk about the why and the how, but first, let's dispel a common myth.

Being polite doesn't make you a doormat.

We've all seen the stereotype: meek and mild librarian/accountant gets walked on by everyone, running others' errands, never getting any respect, until one day, they explode in a rage, baseball bats and fists and profanity flying, and finally, finally, they get the respect they deserve and find true happiness in life.

Let's stop pretending Hollywood represents real life.

First, let's establish some definitions. By 'manners' I mean (as culled from multiple dictionary definitions) "habitual conduct or deportment showing or characterized by correct social usage and marked by an appearance of consideration, tact, deference, or courtesy."

Here's the problem Hollywood has: our 'mannerly' star has focused entirely on the 'deference' portion of that definition, as if manners only (or always) referred to giving others what they want. Showing deference to others is often part of good manners, but if that was it, manners would have no place in business. Business requires a certain reasonable amount of self-interest; more on that later.

Another aspect of the doormat myth, from a specifically business perspective: while consideration, tact, deference, and courtesy might all describe excellent customer service, the 'habitual' part bothers some. You know them; they just know you have to keep an eye on every customer or they'll steal from you; have to hedge on the guarantees or folks will cheat you; and never ever take the customer's word for anything because they're just waiting for a chance to lie to you.

To those folks, manners are only for the cooperative, easy-to-deal-with customers. If the customer falls out of character, this little entrepreneur isn't going to take any guff from a troublemaker.

But that's not what 'habitual' means, and it's not how manners will transform your business.

Let's establish some ground rules.

For the sake of this discussion, we'll assume that your product or service is as good as can be expected. You and your staff are fairly competent. You're not facing some existing fatal flaw, because the best habit of tact and courtesy won't save a bad business.

But being determined to show consideration, tact, deference, and courtesy in every single human contact, direct or indirect, will change your business for the better.

It's not just about what we traditionally consider customer service, either. If the only time your best manners surface is when you're taking a customer's cash, it's fairly obvious where your real interests lie.

Back up a bit.

Lately everyone (including me) is talking about relationship marketing. That implies an ongoing exchange. Both of those words ('ongoing' and 'exchange') are important, and are affected by your manners.

In order to avoid an actively negative experience, your customers and prospects expect two things: accuracy and availability; what I like to call "getting it right" and "getting it out there." Consideration for your customer means you'll extend the courtesy of ensuring that what they get is what they ordered, that it was priced correctly, delivered in good condition, all that stuff. You'll be open hours that make sense to your customers, not just to you. Your employees will look for opportunities to help, and not hide in the stockroom to avoid answering questions.

Your manners set the tone of your business from start to finish in every department, not just on the front line, facing the customer.

In order to create an ongoing positive exchange, your customers would like to participate, and even have you advise them; what I call "give 'em a voice" and "give 'em advice." (Note: the two 'gets' only avoid dissatisfaction; they do not create a positive experience. No one calls a friend to tell them excitedly, "I hired a pool cleaner the other day, and he actually cleaned my pool!")

The participation part may just be the most critical juncture when it comes to how your manners set the tone. The very best marketing is when your customers talk among themselves and to others. Genuine word of mouth, that which wasn't artificially generated, is priceless. And in classic 'birds of a feather' fashion, the people who talk about your business will most likely reflect your manner of dealing with them.

If it's been your habit to give troublesome customers a piece of your mind, fully expect your customers to share a piece of their mind in the most public fashion possible. You will be featured in their "10 things I hate blog", no doubt about it. And in a reflection of the web's organic method of rewarding passion, their diatribe against your perceived lack of consideration, tact, deference, or courtesy is very likely to show up ahead of your company website in web searches. Ouch.

If, on the other hand, your habit is to seek first to understand why a disgruntled customer (or employee, vendor, or partner, for that matter) is thinking the way they do, that willingness to understand will generally be reflected by the folks who choose to do business with you. When they write about you, talk about you, think about you, it will be in terms and imagery which are conducive to an ongoing exchange.

The final consumer need, advice, is the one we're most familiar with as far as manner of presentation: you just know that if you're trying to convince your suspects (those you think should be your customers) or prospects to become customers, you'd better be on your best behaviour. What's not always obvious is that it's good manners and good business to be more proactive than waiting for a warm body to walk into the shop or pick up the phone.

Did you just learn about a new benefit your service can provide? A postcard or letter to those who've already used it can work wonders. Yes, these are folks who've already given you their money. This whole 'ongoing relationship' thing is not about money (did I forget to mention that?) These are people who we hope are already fans. Give them something to talk about to their friends and relatives and neighbors.

And then, don't try to sell them anything. Give them the information with no strings attached, make them feel good all over again about using your services, and then don't pester.

Don't pester. Ever.

If these folks have given you the privilege of an ongoing dialog, don't ever abuse it. Bad manners can kill a dialog in an instant, and with an email or paper dialog, you may not even realize it or be able to discover why it happened.

Get it right. Get it out there. Give 'em a voice. Give 'em advice. If you have genuine consideration for your customers they'll be in the forefront of your mind at every step. And they'll know it.

He Started It!

This is where manners being 'habitual conduct' is hardest—and most critical.

Obviously, it's easy to be nice to folks when they're behaving. Anyone can do that, and nearly everyone does. Being like everyone else is not a way to make your business stand out.

Treating the problem customer with good manners makes good business sense, for all the same reasons that treating the pleasant customer with good manners does. In fact, on different days, your good customer might just be the problem customer.

Remember, we each have an overwhelming need to have our uniqueness acknowledged, even celebrated.

Arguments Cannot Be Won

Earlier, I hope we dispensed with the unpleasant belief that customers are just lining up to lie, cheat, and steal. Rather, like you and I, they're looking for a good product or service at a fair price. If they're unhappy, consider the very real possibility that some part of that expectation wasn't met. Imagine: if you can find out what it was and fix it, it's like getting a free business consultation. Customers who complain are trying to tell you what's broken. Ignoring them, or worse, chasing them away, is like hearing a strange noise from the engine and turning up the radio.

But what about that one customer, the real troublemaker? You warned them not to do this or that, and they did it anyway. Now it's broken or lost or gummed up and they think it's your fault. Honest. They really believe you didn't provide a good product or service at a fair price. They want it made right, even if they're saying so a bit too loudly or not in the most pleasant terms.

You really only have two choices: either make it right, or politely fire them as your customer. Let's talk about the latter first.

If they're truly the irascible type we're talking about, convincing them they're wrong and still keeping them as a customer is not one of your options. You're beyond a friendly debate ending in mutual understanding. You're putting out a fire. It doesn't matter who started it; it matters that you keep the smell of smoke out of your business.

Although I believe it's not as common as some small business operators think, it does occasionally reach the point that you'll be harming your business to keep this customer. If you decide that an ongoing relationship will do more harm than good to both of you, calmly, politely let them know that you've done all you can. Apologize that you haven't been able to make them happy. Express a genuine hope that someone else who offers the same product or service will be able to do what you can't. And that's all.

While it's tempting to send them packing with a flea in their ear, any additional ammunition you give them for their back fence gossip or weblog is foolish.

But consider another possibility. How many times have you said something in the heat of anger and realized later that you were just plain dead wrong? If it wasn't this week, it probably wasn't much longer than that. Unless you're of the very calmest temperament, we all get heated up once in a while.

Consider how your victim's reaction affects your desire to either apologize or acknowledge your culpability. The one who fired it right back at you isn't at the top of the list; the one who seemed more concerned about what was troubling you than about their own feelings will probably be on the receiving end of some world-class groveling.

You might fire that customer, but if you do it right, they just might hire themselves back, and be better citizens next time.

But what if you don't want to fire them? You just reduced your choices from two to one: make it right. Make it right in their eyes, not yours.

It can be expensive, if you're talking about money. We're not, remember? We're talking about the value of an ongoing exchange with the people who make your business possible. Yes, it can be galling to do a job over when you know you did it right; to replace or repair something you know the customer damaged through their own ignorance.

Remember, manners are "habitual conduct or deportment showing or characterized by correct social usage and marked by an appearance of consideration, tact, deference, or courtesy." Any exceptions to a habit can be fatal to that habit. If you're looking at the lifelong benefit of keeping this person as a customer and of their telling others how accommodating you were when the chips were down, making them happy becomes a small price to pay.

It isn't easy, and you shouldn't practice on your toughest customers. Start developing the habit now. Here's one concept that might help.

Your Default Setting

Remember: if you plant flowers, you get flowers. If you plant weeds, you get weeds. If you plant nothing, you get weeds.

Look for what's special, unique, positive about each customer. Otherwise, in the absence of a positive effort to see the good, you'll see their negative traits. The only way to really see what makes this employee or customer special and unique is to actively look for it.

Establish this habit while you're working with the folks who are easy to deal with. It's like cultivating the garden.

Once you've got a field of flowers, dealing with a difficult customer is no harder than dealing with a single weed.

Manners Still Matter

The personality of your business is established more by the personality of its leadership than by any other factor. When it comes to ethics and personality, I fall squarely in the Golden Rule school: treat others as they'd like to be treated, with consideration, tact, deference, and courtesy.

The Golden Rule: "do to others what you would have others do to you." It seems that many really don't understand it. Let's clear that up.

It's Still Golden

I like ice cream. A lot. Especially rocky road.

You may not like rocky road. You may not like ice cream at all. As hard as I find it to believe that, it's possible.

Does the Golden Rule mean that, because I like ice cream, especially rocky road, I should serve it to you? Not at all. What it means is, when I have dessert, I want something I especially like. When I serve you dessert, it should be something **you** especially like. If that's rocky road ice cream, that's great; we'll share. If not, I'd better know you well enough to serve **your** favorite, and not assume it's the same as mine.

The Golden Rule is about consideration, deference, courtesy, selflessness. Contrary to the endless misinterpretations today, it is not flawed. It's still the perfect rule of human interaction: treat others as they desire to be treated.

The Best Policy

At one time it seemed that business operators didn't think about much more than taking your cash. Ethics, the idea that we each have moral duties and obligations, didn't have any real effect on day-to-day business. I'm glad to see that changing. Without honesty your business is a time bomb, just waiting to blow up in your face.

Like so many aspects of business, social, and personal development, the real challenge is consistent application. We all know how easy it is to be honest when there's nothing at stake. We also learn pretty early in life that, sometimes, a little creative storytelling comes in handy.

It's not true.

It's not my goal to indoctrinate you into my personal ethics as far as your personal life. Your business operations are a different matter. In business you absolutely must hold yourself and your employees to an unflinching and absolute commitment to scrupulous honesty.

It's not easy. It can cost money. It can be humiliating if we messed up. It may, temporarily, cause strained relations. But in the long run, just like a healthy diet, honesty is most assuredly the best policy. Your business will become known for it; trust me, when folks know a business operator is honest, business picks up.

It's also easier only having to keep track of one version of what happens in your business. You may know someone who indulged in some creative storytelling, and then forgot who knew the truth, and who only knew the modified version. The results are painful and embarrassing, and can cost trust permanently.

Hard to Earn, Easy to Lose

It takes time and consistent effort to develop a reputation, to earn the trust of clients, employees, and others. There's no shortcut; attempts at shortcuts, in fact, are an excellent way to make the process even longer and more tortuous.

But no matter what the relationship, even if it's lifelong, a single untrustworthy action can reduce it to nothing. Losing trust isn't incremental, the way it's earned. Your emotional bank account can be overdrawn in an instant, and even with a close friend, it can be permanent.

With customers, it's almost certain to be. While taking calculated risks is part of the entrepreneurial spirit, this isn't one of the risks you should ever consider.

Tactful, Not Tacky

Though we've already spent quite a bit of time on the larger picture of social manners, another misconception needs quashing. Honesty, in a social setting, does not equal blunt rudeness.

If your customer asks what you think of their business suggestion, honesty does not require you to bluntly tell them you think it's idiotic. Honesty can always be balanced with tact and kindness. Tact and kindness are good for customer service; bluntness is not.

It's more a matter of how we think than a specific course of action. It's a rare circumstance where there is no response which is both truthful and tactful. What's required is the desire to look for it. Remember our patch of dirt: in the absence of positive effort, it'll grow weeds. If we don't look for what's tactful yet truthful, we'll be tempted to take one of the two easy roads: rudeness or lies. Both are fatal to a business relationship.

See You at Nine

Keeping our word leads nicely to the next personal habit: punctuality. Yup; just plain being on time. It falls squarely in the first two dissatisfaction-eliminating facets of customer service: accuracy and availability.

Punctuality isn't just about being on time for a meeting, although that's critical. It's also about timely delivery, whether by mail or in person. It's about timely response, by phone, email, or smoke signal. We'll come back to that in a bit.

As VAs we need to give realistic estimates of timeframes, then do all we can not just to meet them, but exceed them. That's how word-of-mouth is created, not by simply doing what's expected.

Don't Aggravate Lateness

When I was young, I was always late. I've spent half a lifetime working to develop punctuality and it seems to be improving.

Aggravating the problem was how I handled being late. The lesson I learned when I made this change has led to a major reduction in my business stress.

When I was late, all I did was hurry more to try to be less late. Of course, people were always waiting, and once you're late, being less late than you might have been really doesn't help much. You know what does help?

A phone call.

If you're late, make a phone call. "Sorry, I'm going to be three/five/fifteen minutes late. Your time is valuable, and I'm very sorry I didn't plan better." To date (15 years since I started the habit) the only reaction I ever remember is, "No problem; thanks for letting me know." In fact, I get "No worries; I'm late as well" as often as not.

If you make a mistake (and lateness is a mistake), admit it as soon as you're aware of it and do what you can to fix it. Clients, prospects, even suspects don't expect perfection (if they do, you can't work with them anyway.) They expect mistakes now and then. What they care about is how you deal with the mistake. Of course, they won't excuse incompetence, but you might be surprised how much good will you get by being forthright.

Let the client know up front if for some reason we're going to be late with a project. Apologize, and compensate in some way. It doesn't have to be money! Be creative. Just spice up the apology. You know, candy, flowers, a card— make sure they know you're sincere.

I Hear You Knocking

When someone walks into your coffee shop or computer repair shop, how soon do they expect to be served? Reasonable answers probably range in seconds, or perhaps minutes.

How many of your customers would wait two days in your shop for a latte or a computer cable they needed? How many would wait on hold on the phone overnight?

Communication concepts and expectations are changing. Many people now use email as if it were a telephone; more like instant messaging than sending a letter. The internet has raised the bar, whether we like it or believe it or not. Reality doesn't matter; what matters is your suspect's/prospect's perception, right? (This is another case for judgment, not rigid rules. In the section on 'Getting Things Done', we'll go over keeping email and the telephone in their place.)

How quickly do you reply to queries from your website or in your email? Are they answered as quickly as your telephone? They should be. Immediacy is part of making the sale; you've got their attention—keep it!

An immediate reply is also unexpected; it's remarkable (in two senses: that it's amazing, and it's worth talking about.)

I had a problem with ItsAGrind.com, the website for the It's A Grind chain of coffee houses. It wasn't a big deal, but I'd noticed quirky behaviour more than once when I was trying to find a local shop. As a web developer, I'm more sensitive to what I consider a 'broken' website than some might be, so I submitted some comments about the inconvenience using their web form.

In less than one hour, I received a reply. Not a solution; the bloke who responded wasn't sure what was causing the problem, but assured me someone would look into it. He also mentioned the upcoming launch of their website's redesign.

Less than one hour is most impressive. The fact that it was Marty Cox, the president of It's A Grind, was a pretty fancy topping on the sundae.

Remarkable? Well, I was amazed, and said so. I've also told more than a few people.

It's just common sense: if someone wants to talk to you about your products or services, answering them promptly is the only way to do business. So is prompt delivery; so is punctuality. My policy is to respond to any request within 24 hours. Usually, though, my response is within the hour. Even if the task can't be started right away, the client receives confirmation that their email or call was received and that their project is on your radar.

Why We're Like This

It's almost impossible to avoid seeing a timepiece almost everywhere you look. Nearly every adult in some countries wears a wrist watch. Your cell phone's display probably includes a readout of the time. Right down there in the corner of my computer screen is another. Driving down the street, even if you didn't have another clock on the dashboard you'd hear the time announced on the radio at least once an hour.

We're a society obsessed with timekeeping. So how on earth can anyone ever be late?

It's pretty obviously not about time. Less obviously, maybe, is that it's about manners.

Here's my confession. When I was young, the reason I was always late was because I was arrogant and selfish.

My chronic lateness had two sources: I never really wanted to stop what I was already doing to get to what I was supposed to be doing, but worse, I honestly believed others weren't as important as me. There I was, doing something really meaningful, and if we started the next thing 15 minutes late, I was sure they didn't mind waiting.

It took years of unpleasant interaction and a major change in my self-image to decide that punctuality was a way of showing my consideration for others. Of course, first I had to have that consideration.

Those of us who are chronically late fall into a handful of personality types defined by psychologists, but the short version is that if we're chronically late, we don't respect others; we don't think they're as important as we are. Dale

Carnegie is not impressed, and neither are those you do business with.

When others realize that you don't value their time it's a short step to thinking you don't value them—and an even shorter step to them not valuing you.

If you know you have a problem with punctuality, treat it like any other gap you might discover in your professional abilities, and patch it. We've discussed learning types: if you can read a book and get the concepts, check your local library or search the internet for resources. If you're the type who can enlist the aid of friends to make the change, do it. If you've tried before and can't seem to overcome the lateness habit, consider finding a life skills coach to help you sort out causes and solutions.

And, those of you who are glad I'm not talking to you right now, try one of these experiments:

- keep a log of your punctuality for a week or so; prove it to yourself in writing
- ask a trusted friend or business associate if you have a reputation for punctuality

Hopefully, you won't find any surprises. If you do, come back and read this section again; it's more meaningful once your eyes are open.

Social Skills

Speech

We're surrounded by the sounds of speech. It's such a part of the fabric of life that most of us don't give it a second thought (or even a first thought.) Other than baby's first words or the fear associated with public speaking, very few of us think about our speech.

If we're swimming in a sea of speech, I think it deserves some attention. If you speak while conducting business, you may agree.

The core value underpinning business speech is graciousness: actively saying and doing what makes others comfortable around us, and avoiding that which doesn't. It's one more place where, without positive effort, we'll get weeds—mistakes in speech are the easiest mistakes to make.

Yes, Sir; No, Ma'am

Balancing friendliness and formality is crucial to making your clientele comfortable. Many languages have different syntax to indicate when we're chatting with friends and when we're addressing royalty. On the other hand English, especially as spoken in the United States, tends strongly toward a single level of formality (informality, actually.)

Anthropologists refer to 'high context' and 'low context' cultures. In low context situations, meaning is tied closely to the actual words we use. In high context, much of a statement's meaning is derived from other signals.

When others are speaking to you, be aware of the messages being sent by both words and the social context (facial expression, tone of voice and volume, eye direction, physical proximity, etc.) How does it feel; are you comfortable? If not, why?

If you've never given much thought to how your speech affects others, it can be tough to get a handle on. If your speech makes prospects or customers uncomfortable, they're not likely to give you feedback; they'll just go elsewhere. If there's a friend or acquaintance who seems to get this right and who you trust to give you honest feedback, ask for it. Sometimes, though, it makes sense to bring in professional help. Many life coaches and business coaches can give you meaningful feedback on your social skills, and advice on what to adjust and how.

There's No Such Thing as Too Little Profanity

If your goal is to make suspects, prospects, and customers comfortable, profanity is incredibly risky. Have you ever heard of someone walking out of a movie or putting down a best-selling book, saying "There just wasn't enough swearing!" On the other hand, there are plenty of people who'll avoid you if you make them uncomfortable with your word choice.

Every culture has different perspectives on what's considered profane or vulgar speech, but you can do your own test: would you say it in front of your neighbor's little kids, your grandmother, your religious advisor, the President/Queen/other head of state? No? Then don't say it in the hearing of a customer.

No one is going to refuse to do business with you because you don't use profanity. But if they hear salty speech behind the counter, through the stockroom door, or coming out of your delivery truck, somewhere along the line someone will be offended. They probably won't mention it. They'll just take their business elsewhere. This is one more risk you just don't have to take.

Say It Loud, Say It Clear

While we were in Ireland a couple years ago we had more than one interesting communication issue. I've heard tell that even folks from Dublin have a hard time with the powerful brogue of the west counties. With my lifelong exposure to Irish, English, and Scottish accents, I did okay, but my daughter had an experience in a pub in Galway that's a staple in her storytelling.

When we walked into the pub, there was a gent at the door who had clearly arrived early to get a good start on his beverage consumption. He wasn't overly familiar or in any way unpleasant, but between the brogue and the Guinness, none of us could understand a single word he said. Being the only Yanks in the pub, he wanted to be friendly and chat, and since our daughter is a gorgeous redhead, he quite naturally elected her as our spokesman.

After the eleventh time she'd said, "Excuse me?" she gave up. For the rest of the evening, if he said something and laughed, she laughed right along with him; if the look on his face made it clear this was a pronouncement of doom, she shook her head slowly, making it clear she understood his concern. Or anger. Or whatever it was.

Your customers aren't likely to take home a similar story about the interesting chap from the computer store. "We didn't understand a *word* he said, so we bought everything in the store!" Theoretically, you're talking because what you're saying has some importance. Speak clearly, and loud enough to be heard comfortably. If there's background noise, be aware of it. (If you can reduce it by turning off a radio or equipment or by closing a door, do so.)

Again, feedback from others is really helpful. You know what you're saying; the curse of knowledge makes you almost useless as your own speech analyst. (If you can record yourself talking and play it back later, it helps somewhat.)

Here's where a group like Toastmasters or other public speaking training can really help. It doesn't mean you have to actually do any public speaking, but most of the folks in these organizations do, and they know what it takes to get yourself heard intelligibly.

Phone

Speaking on the telephone carries the same caveats as speaking in person, with a few extras: it's even more important to watch your word choice when there's no facial expression or much other social context for what you're saying.

Even if you have a great website, answer email queries religiously, and have lots of walk-in traffic, you can't ignore your phone skills. While the details of working in a call center or succeeding in a primarily telephone-based business would fill a book (and probably have; check the recommended reading list) here are some basics:

- answer promptly
- speak clearly, and loud enough to be heard
- identify yourself; more on that below
- listen very carefully; more on that below, too
- consider the 'Hold' button your last option, not your first
- consider speaker phones a non-option; speaker phones are evil—they pick up strange electronic sounds, they make you sound like you're in a tin can, and they make it obvious to the caller that their voice is being broadcast into whatever space you're in (which they can't see)
- use good equipment and services; your clear voice is the only emotional connection the prospect is making with your business while you're on the phone

· be aware of others near you; don't overwhelm their conversations with your volume, and don't let local noises or voices confuse or annoy your caller

Callers are often thinking about something else when you answer the phone, especially if you answer promptly. (When I spent a lot of time on the phone in previous businesses, I'm pretty sure I could have answered the phone "City Zoo; this is the gorilla" and most callers wouldn't have even noticed. Don't ask me why I know this.) Be gracious; if you say the name of your business or your own name, don't be surprised if they miss it. During the conversation, find a way to reintroduce yourself.

Humans are very visual creatures. When you're on the phone, it's easy to be distracted by what you see. Don't let it happen. Your caller will know you're not listening, and what you miss could mean losing a sale or a customer. Keep a notepad near every phone and take notes. That way, what your eyes are taking in is related to what's happening on the phone.

If your business is growing, avoid electronic answering devices, phone trees and the like for as long as you can. Besides postponing yet another technical hassle, nothing says "Welcome" like a human voice.

Voice Mail

Unless you provide an urgency-related service or have a sizable team of employees, you probably don't answer your business phone 24 hours a day. If callers are going to get your voice mail machine or service, here are a few tips to help you not aggravate unnecessarily:

· speak clearly, and loud enough to be heard (have I said this enough?)
· identify your business

- if your equipment offers this option, tell callers how they can skip this message in the future
- include answers to your most frequent after-hours questions: hours of operation, address, whatever folks call about endlessly (put all this on your website, too, of course)
- check voice mail **before the start of business** in the morning and make sure calls are returned **before** people feel they have to call again

The telephone is a nearly zero-context communication device; your caller can't see your face, has no idea what that noise is in the background, and isn't aware that you have four people in line. Realizing that they're essentially operating blind can help you keep them comfortable by what you communicate, and how.

Email

I mentioned earlier that business email should be answered promptly, and we covered communication mirroring. While email is one of the foundations of business in the internet age, it has one very high risk.

If the telephone is a low-context communication method, email is even lower. In email, the emotional context always downgrades. If you write something in a straightforward manner it will sound blunt. If you're blunt, it will sound like you're enraged. Subtlety is hard to capture in email (or in any written communication; just ask a writer.)

For normal business communication, this means choosing your words carefully, and infusing messages with more warmth and friendliness than you might use in speech.

Whenever possible, and keeping in mind communication mirroring, don't use email for important conversations. We've all heard horror stories of employees being fired via email. And I will never forget the enthusiastic email I sent to my supervisor at one company—which got me called on the carpet for being antagonistic and negative. Re-reading the email it wasn't nearly so obvious that I'd had a smile on my lips and a song in my heart when I sent it. Had I simply stepped around the corner to his office and let him see my face when I said it, there would have been no confusion.

Again, reams have been written about email etiquette. Err on the side of courtesy, and substitute face-to-face or at least telephone communication if there's any possibility of emotional volatility in your message.

Let's remember we're professionals—business owners. This isn't the place to become sloppy, lazy or use text messaging shortcuts. The appearance of our emails to clients should be similar to a business letter. If you're going to err, err on the side of formality.

Appearance

There is no Reality; Only Perception, Part II

As we discussed earlier, you don't get to choose how others perceive you. We all make snap judgments about others; we notice how they're dressed, their personal hygiene, their facial expression. Much of that judgment is subconscious.

Long ago when I washed windows for a living I thought it odd that, if I did my work correctly, it was invisible. The only thing anyone would see would be the mistakes.

Your appearance should play the same role in your business. Even if you're working remotely, you will occasionally meet clients and prospects in person. If they can't help but notice how you're dressed or if their attention is drawn to some aspect of your hygiene, something is wrong.

There is an endless list of personal choice when it comes to attire; discussing personal hygiene can be a minefield. My goal here is not to dispense my opinion on dress or give offense about personal hygiene, but to help ensure that it has at least been considered.

Clothes

Whether you realize it or not, when you see a man in neatly creased slacks with a little horsey on his shirt and another in jeans with the name of a rock band on **his** shirt, you make mental judgments and comparisons of their income and importance. In the western world, we associate certain types of dress with certain levels of wealth.

The tendency these days is toward casual attire. On the same day you can see folks in the grocery store in what looks like pajamas, kids with their pants halfway down their legs, and jeans in every possible stage of decomposition. How people dress is their own business—until it comes to business. Then, your work clothing is marketing, just like the sign out front.

Creating the correct mental impression with suspects, prospects, and customers is just as important as properly describing the attributes of your newest line of widgets. If you are conscious of the role money plays in business and respect your customers and yourself, your attire should reflect that.

It's always safer to err on the side of caution with clothing. Dress a little better than others might expect. If they walk into your computer repair shop expecting sloganized t-shirts and jeans, and instead see polo shirts and creased dress slacks, they will notice. If they walk into your coffee shop expecting polo shirts and dress slacks and see a dress shirt and tie, again, they'll notice.

Of course, it doesn't make sense to go to extremes; if you're working on a client's car in a tuxedo, unless you're intentionally creating a remarkable marketing statement (a 'purple cow') you'll simply look foolish. Dressing just a little better than expected has the best effect.

My Shirt is My Opinion

Unless your personal opinion on a non-business topic plays a role in your business, think twice before expressing it on your clothes or with jewelry, tattoos, whatever. Others, not surprisingly, may not share your views on politics, religion, music, child rearing, or any number of subjects. Unless you're willing to risk offense, don't one-sidedly proclaim your support for this or disdain for that during a business transaction. If it wouldn't be an appropriate part of the current business conversation, don't say it silently either.

Modesty

The children's photography studio where my daughter works has a dress code, but it goes beyond white shirt/black slacks and shoes. The manager makes it clear that, because they're in an environment completely catering to families, modesty is part of the dress code. If the skin of your lower back is visible when you bend to pick something up, you'll be sent home to change. If the neckline is too low or the pants too tight, same thing.

In this day and age this might seem extreme. But as I wrote earlier about word choice, while no one is likely to be offended by modest clothing, the opposite can't be said. If someone comes with their significant other to your place of business and the employee helping them is dressed provocatively you're risking offense. It's a risk you just don't have to take.

Non-Clothing Attire

I keep referring to 'clothing', but appearance is certainly more than just the clothes we wear. Hair, makeup, jewelry, piercings, tattoos; if it's attached to us and others see it, it's part of our attire.

I'll dispense with my personal comments on piercings and tattoos first: the only time I was ever tempted to get a tattoo, I asked myself if I owned even one item of clothing I'd want to wear, day in and day out, for the rest of my life. I have no tattoos. (The same conversation happened regarding the very cool pirate piercing for my left ear, which also never happened.)

I'll emphasize again that we're not discussing personal preference or lifestyle; we're talking about your appearance in your business.

These other items of attire can mostly be dealt with in the same way as your clothing: don't shock or surprise folks, and whenever possible, be a little more formal than they expect. (That absolutely rules out the 'just rolled out of bed look' for hair, by the way.) With these non-clothing parts of our attire 'formal' should include 'subtle' as well.

It may come as a surprise to some younger readers, but not everyone appreciates multiple facial piercings and large tattoos. If you're dedicated to only doing business with other pierced and tattooed folks, they're certainly appropriate if you choose to have them. But if you're going to operate a business which hopes to attract customers a little older than you, and especially if you're hoping to attract those who are slightly more wealthy: be advised that many older or more conservative folks are repelled by such things. They will find someone else to do business with. It will not matter how talented or inexpensive or fast you are.

Cleanliness

The modern trend toward casual attire has been accompanied by lax attitudes about cleanliness. It can be fatal to a business relationship.

Your Person

Let's get past the hard part first: if you want to succeed in business of any kind, you absolutely must be physically clean. The need for daily bathing may seem obvious, but if you walk through any crowded shopping mall your nose will tell you otherwise.

Smell is an incredibly evocative sense. If customers notice any unpleasant odors when they're doing business with you, they'll be uncomfortable. That doesn't just mean brushing your teeth regularly and not eating garlic at lunch; if your perfume, cologne, or hair treatment is overpowering it's only slightly less unpleasant than being too close to someone who hasn't bathed recently.

Just as there is no excuse for rudeness, there is no excuse for lack of personal cleanliness. Don't ever let lax habits damage your reputation as a professional.

Your Environment

Cleanliness is most noticeable when it's absent. It's another place where, unless you run a service station on the interstate, no one is going to mention how clean your shop is or how clean your clothing is. If it's not clean, you're taking another one of those unnecessary risks.

It isn't only important in the food service industry. I worked with a plumber years ago whose nickname in a nearby affluent community was 'Mr. Clean' because when he left a job, the only way you knew he'd been there was that the plumbing wasn't broken any more. No drywall dust on the floor where a wall had to be cut open; no old plumbing parts for the customer to dispose of; no grease or smelly liquids or anything anywhere it wasn't supposed to be.

It's no surprise that to this day, he continues to have more work than he can do, despite charging a premium price for his services.

Prospects look through your windows as they walk toward your shop. They see the delivery or service van. The look at the chair they sit on, the table they eat off or rest their arms or books on. They notice the magazines in the waiting room and the signs hanging on the doors and in the windows. They absolutely notice your restrooms. Make sure they're all just a little nicer than your customers expect.

Your business will reflect you. Your customers, however, want it to reflect them, too. Make sure they like what they see.

Chapter Three: Getting Things Done

As with the rest of this book, this chapter is more about how you think and less about the nuts and bolts of time or project management. I'm not going to tell you which computer program will solve your problems or how to organize your business by making meaningful to-do lists.

While you definitely need tools to effectively set and achieve goals, that's just what they are: tools. While having the right tool can make a job easier, having the tool isn't what gets the job done any more than buying a hammer and level will get a picture hung in the living room.

If you understand some of the basic concepts of planning, prioritizing, and performing, and have some warning about potential pitfalls, you'll be in a much better position to select the tools which will work best for you and your business. The fact is that there is no 'best' tool; as I've said endlessly, we're each unique and a one-size-fits-all solution is really a doesn't-fit-anyone solution.

This chapter will be separated rather loosely into planning concepts, setting priorities, and performing—the part where you actually get things done. It's also aimed primarily at those of us who weren't born organized, but have to struggle a little to stay on top of it all. (That includes me. A lot.)

But first, let's chat about some general concepts which will apply to all of it.

To Tell or Not To Tell?

Anyone who's ever tried to lose weight (again) or change some habit (again) has faced the question of whether telling others provides helpful support or just an opportunity for frustration. The answer is that it depends on who you tell.

Among your acquaintances are those people who will hear about your new project (or revival of an old project) and immediately let you know why you're going to fail. You probably already know who they are.

Don't tell them. They'll figure it out for themselves when you succeed.

But there's another group, hopefully a large one, who will be pleased that you're sharing your goals and dreams with them. They'll want to understand what you're doing and why, and they'll have advice. They'll always have advice. Listen to it. Maybe you already knew whatever they're sharing, maybe you disagree with it, maybe it's something new. But when you have folks on your side, keep them there. When you get emotional support from people who believe in you, however slightly, latch onto it and make the most of it. It's worth more than any technical tool you'll find.

The Short Answer is There's No Short Answer

For those of us who struggle to be effective, to get tasks and projects done, to turn our dreams into reality, the biggest win will be about habits. There's a reason Stephen Covey's book is called 'The 7 *Habits* of Highly Effective People.' Those effective people have learned that the things you do without having to stop and think will determine your real direction and speed.

Habits don't change over night. Habits develop over time, so it's going to take time and persistence to make the new habits of effectiveness stick.

Tools and Habits You Will Need

There are a few tools you're going to need which are so universal that I think I can recommend them.

The first one is good reading skills. The second is good writing skills. The third is solid math skills. Sorry.

While I realize that many of us are doing just fine in these areas, my experience is that most small business owners have noticeable shortcomings in one or more. Before we move on to the psychology of getting things done, let's establish the fact that you can't ignore these now any more than you tried to back in school. I'll try to make it as painless as possible.

Reading Well, and Often

Educators tell us that children who learn to read well when they're young have an easier time learning. For my money, reading is still the most important self-training method. Reading is involved in multiple aspects of virtually any business. As a small business operator, you're wearing so many hats that avoiding the need to read well just isn't possible.

Reading develops verbal skills, promotes patience, and stimulates your imagination. If you're wrestling with business issues, which of those isn't helpful?

Without good reading comprehension, you won't get the details out of instructions, shipping manifests, contracts, self-help books, email or a myriad of other written documentation. It's been said that anyone who *doesn't* read is no better off than someone who *can't* read. There's a reason writing has been a primary form of communication for six thousand years. Written material can last millennia. It's fairly simple to create, duplicate, and deliver.

If you're not currently an avid reader, it's just possible you never will be one of those folks who just love to curl up with a good book. That's okay; some of our business skills aren't what we'd choose for recreation. It doesn't excuse us from being good at them. There are many ways to improve your reading. I'll include some suggestions here. Others are included in the 'Resources' section of the book.

The first step toward being a better reader and getting more out of what you read is to do it more often. Practice. Works with everything else; works with reading, too. If you can read, you can read better. Reading requires conscious effort. It can't be done without thinking.

Recognize that reading isn't about getting through the words, it's about understanding the message. Read with purpose. Know why you're reading something and it can change from a meaningless chore to a meaningful business task.

Reading is a dance between your eyes and your brain. Generally, adding your mouth to the dance confuses things. Most of us speak at about 120 words per minute, but good reading comprehension takes place at about twice that. If you move your lips when you're reading you slow down. It makes it difficult to absorb the ideas, and easier to get stuck on just the words.

Reading well is also a fundamental key to writing well.

Writing Well

While I flatter myself that you're enjoying reading this because I'm a good writer, I'm well aware that I fall short of the ideal writer in many ways. I hope you'll find a balance between style and mechanics in your own writing.

As with reading, there are loads of resources to help with your writing. Before I list a handful of my favorite simple writing concepts, consider why writing well is so important to your business: marketing materials, instructions and procedures, letters, website content and more require not just that you write, but that you write well. As with many areas, if you have shortcomings in this area, clients, prospects and suspects aren't likely to speak up. They'll simply adjust their opinion of you.

Writing, like reading, takes practice. You can't do anything well if you don't do it often; ask any musician or sports enthusiast. One simple way to write more is to have a weblog. Write *something* every single day.

One of the best helps in writing is a willing friend who's already good at it. Having someone you trust read what you've written can help isolate spelling, grammar and punctuation errors you may not even be aware of. Keeping track of your most common problems will help correct them.

Another resource I'll urge you to keep handy is "The Elements of Style" by Strunk and White. Some of the tips on this list are condensed from that short book. It is a vital resource for anyone who writes, which includes virtually all business people.

Some tips to help avoid an amateurish appearance to your writing:

·   Learn which apostrophes are superfluous and which aren't—An apostrophe tells the reader that letters have been left out, or points out possession. Just because a word ends in 's' doesn't mean it needs an apostrophe. Acronyms are a common place folks get tripped up. VCRs and TVs are plurals; no apostrophe needed. Before you add an apostrophe simply ask yourself: are there letters left out, such as in "can't" or "won't"? Is one thing owned by another, as in "a dog's breakfast" ? If not, you can generally forget the apostrophe. The tricky exception is "its" and "it's"—this is the one case where the apostrophe is only used for the contraction, not the possessive. If you're saying "it is", then "it's" but if you're referring to the dog's breakfast then write "its breakfast" with no apostrophe.

·   Learn to use commas, semicolons, colons and periods— Do some research online or in "The Elements of Style" for the best effect.

·   Use definite, specific concrete language—Vagueness makes you sound indecisive. This is not a good business skill.

- Omit needless words—Guilty as charged. My greatest shortcoming as a writer is blather. Brevity creates punch you just don't get with wordiness.

- Exclamation marks are for exclamations, not declarations—Please! Adding more exclamation marks to a simple statement won't make more people buy your product or service. If you wouldn't shout it, don't add an exclamation mark when you write it.

- Have someone edit your writing and make a list of your own commonly misused words and expressions.

- Don't overwrite, don't overstate, don't be over familiar—Exaggeration isn't good business writing. Speak to your readers (even in a brief advertisement or weblog post) as honored guests, and you'll fill that huge unmet emotional need to feel special and important. Most of us don't like the artificial familiarity often associated with a used car salesman in a cheap suit. Avoid it in your writing.

- Don't use 133t speak or other unorthodox spelling—Although 'thru' has become familiar through use, it still doesn't look professional. Unless you're writing for teenagers, don't write like a teenager. Even then, use caution. If you do it wrong you're doomed. Swapping in numbers and symbols for letters may look cool to kids but it's no way to appeal to a broad age range.

- Write out abbreviations and acronyms on the first usage—You might think it's obvious that 'CA' means California but many Canadians would beg to differ. Don't assume your readers know what an abbreviation or acronym means unless it has entered the language as a word, like NASA or radar. Feel free to mention that you use Pressurized Uniform Gauging (PUG) and then refer to PUG for the rest of the article, advertisement, instruction or document.

Sue's Thoughts On Basic Writing Skills

Like everyone else, I always wanted to write a book. Yet I never considered myself a writer. Sure I know about good grammar, punctuation and spelling. Does that make me a good writer? It certainly helps!

Unfortunately today many young people graduate from school without a good solid foundation in the basic skills of writing, grammar, punctuation and spelling. So many people now use shortcuts in text messages, emails and on forums that they seem to have forgotten that looking professional in business is vital.

Many clients I've worked with want help with proofreading and editing. They ask me to pay attention to details. They are tired of working with assistants that allow correspondence or emails to go out to customers with spelling and grammar errors.

So make sure you proofread and use correct grammar and spelling. If writing is not your expertise, don't market yourself as a writer. One of my pet peeves is that I often receive marketing materials from other virtual assistants that is full of grammar and spelling errors and that doesn't flow well. If at all possible, ask someone else to proofread for you. Another set of eyes never hurts.

Math is Critical. It Can Even Be Fun. Honest.

While it may be obvious that you need to be able to count and do simple arithmetic to be in business, unless you have more than a passing familiarity with mathematics you leave yourself open to pitfalls.

Knowing how numbers really work with each other and how they're related to the real world gives you a different perspective on so many things. It's a lot like driving through a familiar neighborhood: if you know more streets and landmarks, you give yourself more options for travel. You also have a much better chance of finding your way if you're forced out of familiar paths for some reason.

Sometimes Math isn't About Numbers

Folks who aren't all warm and fuzzy about numbers are more likely to make logical errors while being mathematically accurate. It's easy to focus so hard on adding 1.3 plus 2.4 that you forget that 1.3 cups of sugar plus 2.4 cups of water does not equal 3.7 cups of soggy sugar. (I'll wait while you go try it. Round up some lemons while you're out and we'll have lemonade.)

More extreme versions of innumeracy (a word coined by author John Allen Poulos as the title of his excellent book on numerical illiteracy) can confuse us about what really constitutes a 'rare' occurrence. For instance, draw a dozen Scrabble letters out of a bag. The chances that you can spell a word using some or all of the letters is incredibly high; almost guaranteed.

But what if you choose the word in advance? Ah; now the chances drop to near zero. The difference is between *some* event happening (we can spell a word) and a *specific* event happening (we can spell 'mouse.')

How Many? How Long? How Often?

Years ago I worked for a friend doing landscaping. The project he was starting when he hired me involved removing quite a bit of concrete and replacing it with grass and plants. Hard work, but certainly a worthwhile effort.

He'd rented a roll-off dumpster; basically, the back of a dump truck which they left at the site and took away to the dump after you filled it.

When I arrived on the site for the first time, I was struck by how small the dumpster looked on that great expanse of concrete. Some quick math in my head told me that we were going to fill it about a dozen times, not just once. Not what was contracted for with the removers. We filled it once, sent it away, and found a truck we could use to make repeated trips to the dump.

It ate a chunk out of the profits, cost time, and generally looked unprofessional. I was immediately assigned to measure and verify all estimates before they were delivered to prospective clients after that. (And the contractor and I are still friends, even though I've shared this story.)

Learn to have a mental representation of very large numbers. How long is a thousand seconds? How far is two hundred feet? How much would a million grains of sand weigh? How much space would it take up?

Knowing that the block wall in your warehouse has about 1,000 blocks, that the street in front of your house is about 250 inches wide or that your daily walk around the block takes about 500 steps can help you realize when numbers seem out of step with reality.

Once again, it's easy to just do some math and make assumptions which don't match reality. If you can make 20 phone calls in one hour, how long will it take to make 200? The answer in real life is not ten hours, especially if you're trying to manage your real life and other clients at the same time.

How Accurate is That Measurement?

Statistics are a great way to get a picture of the world around us, and see change. The thing is, it's easy to get all wrapped up on the numbers and forget what's behind them. Since your computer or calculator will let you calculate an number to eleven places to the right of the decimal point, it's tempting to think we can really be that accurate.

Isn't it great when unemployment goes down, for instance? Let's look at two recent years in California. In 2005, the unemployment rate (according to the Bureau of Labor Statistics) was 5.4%. In 2006 it was only 4.9%. H'ray! This might give you the impression something good happened.

Let's talk about a statistical thing called 'margins for error.' It's rare for statistics to be perfectly accurate. Statisticians include a measurement for how close the reported figures really are. Unless you know what that measurement is, the statistics can be meaningless. In our example, suppose we had a margin for error of 1% of the overall sample (I have no idea; I can't find it on their website.) That would mean unemployment in 2005 was between 4.4% and 6.4% and in 2006 it was between 3.9% and 5.9%.

That means it's possible that from 2005 to 2006, unemployment could have grown 1.5% rather than decreasing 0.5%.

If you're measuring increases or decreases in this, that, and the other thing, be aware of how accurate the statistics really are. It's okay if they're just 'really close' as long as you realize it. Writing more numbers after the decimal point doesn't make them real.

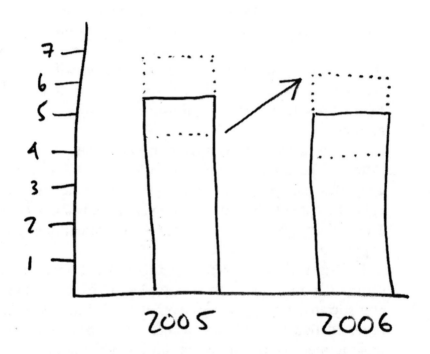

Don't Average Averages

If you track anything by averages, don't make a very, very common mathematical mistake.

Let's say you track average dollars per order of widgets and bongos each quarter. Mid-year, you want to compare, to see which has the higher average dollars per order.

Here are the numbers for Q1:

	# of Orders	Avg $ per Order
Widgets	200	$30
Bongos	100	$29

And Q2:

	# of Orders	Avg $ per Order
Widgets	100	$40
Bongos	200	$39

Widgets had higher average dollars per order each quarter. So if we average the quarterly averages for average dollars per order we get:

	Avg $ per Order
Widgets:	$35
Bongos:	$34

That's wrong. Don't average averages. Accumulate, then average.

	# Orders	Total $	Avg $ per Order
Widgets	300	$10,000	$33.33
Bongos	300	$10,700	$35.67

Habits and Persistence

In order to establish a solid foundation of reading, writing and math habits or to integrate the other ideas from this chapter into your business life, persistence is indispensable.

Everyone seems to love making plans. It's fun to doodle some sketches and write to-do lists, to imagine what it's going to be like when you're done. Some of us really love firing up the project management software and filling in all the tasks and precedents and resources and seeing all that work that's going to be done.

Doing that work is an entirely different matter. There's a reason the Chinese proverb says that the longest journey begins with a single step—beginning is half the battle; maybe more than half.

Planning

Progress is movement toward a goal. No goal, no progress.

Sometimes you get to choose your goal: reduce costs, improve employee morale (including your own), become famous. Other times a goal is thrust upon you: resolve this problem or face a fine or legal sanction; correct that situation or lose an important client, employee or piece of equipment. We'll discuss priorities in a moment and spend some time on the decision making process, for when we have the luxury of setting our own goals on our own terms. For now, let's assume you have an end result in mind, whether it's a project taking weeks or months, or a shorter task you've been putting off because you're not sure how to tackle it.

One of many implementation and efficiency tools in the manufacturing world is called Six Sigma. The name refers to statistical methods of removing variances which cause inefficiency. Yeah, for the average small business operator it's as complicated as it sounds. But the basic process still applies, and it's fairly easy to describe.

The Steps of Progress

The five steps I'm going to talk about are
- Define
- Measure
- Analyze
- Improve
- Control

Define

In 1707, over a thousand sailors drowned off the Isles of Scilly because they didn't know how far east or west they were of land. It's not that they thought it was unimportant; they knew it was a life and death matter. But at the time, there just wasn't a practical method for measuring longitude. Not being able to measure something is just as bad as not knowing it exists or is important.

The first step in getting things done is to properly define the goal. Know what problem you're trying to solve. You'd be amazed (or perhaps not) how often business folks spend time and effort solving the wrong problem. Know what's really broken. Know what will really fix it. If you can't explain both briefly in fairly simple terms to someone who knows nothing about your business, you probably don't fully understand the problem or your proposed solution. Mull it over. Sleep on it. Look at it again. But get to the point that you can explain to someone outside your industry what the problem is, and how you're going to solve it, doing so in a manner that makes sense to them. If you can do that, you've got the problem defined.

Measure

While manufacturers and retailers live by statistics, most service related small businesses don't have statistics on their processes. Most have never measured how long this takes or how often they have to replace that.

Just like progress is movement toward a goal, it is movement *from* a real place. You have to know what that real place is. Don't go with your gut. It didn't work with longitude.

Consider, for instance, the goal of increasing sales per customer. You know that selling more to existing customers is better than converting more prospects into customers.

Do you know how much your customers are spending now? If not, how will you know if it increases? It sounds like a simple question, but the entire advertising industry is based on the commonplace occurrence of making efforts to improve an aspect of your business without measuring it, before or after.

Proper measurements can feel pretty tedious: timing things, tracking numbers, calculating, averaging and other math stuff. But again, don't go with your gut. If your gut was right, you wouldn't have anything to improve. Trust me, if you don't make the effort to get it right this early in the game, you'll have a really hard time sticking with it when things actually are difficult.

Analyze

Here's the fun part. This is the 'planning' part of planning. Look at your measurements, the 'where we are now' picture. Consider where you want to be. Remember, goals should be a stretch, but reachable.

Put real numbers to it; something like
- Current average sales per client: $100
- Proposed average sales per client: $120

Knowing whether that 20% increase is reasonable is partly instinct (yes, this is where you finally get to go with your gut to some extent.) It's also partly a product of the iterative nature of this system. You may end up adjusting your goal up or down as you move toward it. Yes; goals can move. Progress may be movement toward a goal, but that doesn't mean goals never change.

Note that we haven't yet decided how we're going to reach that goal. We've simply decided, for now, what it is.

Improve

This phase includes two parts: how to do it, and doing it.

This is where bringing in outside thinking becomes the most important. Your current thinking patterns and habits are more than likely a contributing factor in the status quo. That's not blame; it's just a fact. A new perspective, a different set of eyes, can really help get a clearer picture. As I've mentioned, there is no reality, only perception. In this case, your reality can be hard to get around. Try to see someone else's reality.

This doesn't necessarily mean a paid consultant. Look around for entrepreneurial organizations in your area.

Check with SCORE or your local small business association. A trusted friend outside your business (maybe the one you were talking to in the 'define' phase above) can often see things just differently enough to help find the path.

Brainstorming, done right, is excellent. The problem most organizations have with brainstorming is that, while you can't control a real storm, brainstorming sessions quickly become analysis and defense sessions. When you're brainstorming, don't analyze any idea; don't reject or even ponder them. Just list them. Go back afterwards and seriously consider each one. Some are patently ridiculous in the light of day, but sometimes an idea that would have been easy to shoot down in the heat of the moment shows real merit when you've let it simmer for a while.

While you're deciding how to approach the problem, keep in mind that you're not likely to find the perfect solution on your first try. If it was that easy, wouldn't you already be there? What you're looking for is a fairly reasonable method of making a measurable improvement on the problem at hand.

Then, experiment. In our example above, increasing sales to existing clients, consider a number of alternatives. Settle on one, and experiment. Try it out for a while. Or ask your clients what would motivate them. Everyone has an opinion; make it clear you want to hear theirs. Once those floodgates are open you'll have all the ideas you can handle.

And measure. Otherwise, how will you know if you're moving toward your goal? How will you know when you get there?

Control

Finally, as anyone who's ever lost weight or replaced an unwanted habit can tell you, it's easy to slip back into old habits. The control phase is your plan to keep the new habits in place.

Once you've sorted out how to increase average sales, make sure the new process is included in employee training. Put it in your customer satisfaction checklist. Create processes which will keep the new habits in place, and which will let you know when something slips. Yes, keep measuring. Not as often as during the earlier phases, but regular measurements are the only way to know whether your hard-won goal is still won.

Don't Overdo It

With all that said, don't overdo the whole planning thing. It's easy to get bogged down when planning is difficult and easy to be distracted when it's fun. Too much planning prevents progress.

In the early stages of launching a new service or making a large change in how you do business, planning needs to have an element of vagueness to it. Too much detail at this point forces you to make important decisions when you have the least amount of information available.

Keep your plans loose enough to adjust, adapt and evolve as you learn more about the problem and your proposed solution along the way. Don't fret about writing things in stone. Consider all decisions temporary. Know when you make them that they could change tomorrow based on new information or understanding.

And finally, don't waste time on problems you don't have yet. When I gave my very first public presentation for my consulting business, a friend loaned me his conference room. We had comfortable space for about a dozen people, and I worried where we would put the overflow. Well, there was none, and if there had been, we would have found a way to deal with it. I'm not suggesting you ignore those rivers and deserts you may have to cross. But if your road doesn't even go there, don't waste time making plans you don't need.

Priorities

Whether it's choosing which one of many projects to work on or just sorting out what you're going to do today, one way or another you need to set priorities. This is a key place those of us with too much to do can get bogged down. I wrote earlier about how having too many choices makes decisions difficult. Having too many tasks or projects is the same, but with a little added pressure.

In the absence of effort, you don't get flowers or even bare dirt; you get weeds. Not setting intelligent priorities is a great way to get weeds.

My father used to tell this story:

Little Johnny was late to school. When his teacher asked why, he said, "I had to run beside my bicycle all the way here."
"But why didn't you just ride your bicycle, Johnny?"
"Because I didn't have time to stop and get on."

If you don't set priorities, it's remarkably easy to put "get to school" ahead of "get on the bicycle."

As you go through your business day, how many little annoyances would disappear if you paused and changed the process, used better tools, or trained someone who would really enjoy the task? We all know that single effort to repair, reorganize, or train will pay itself back many times over, but we put it off because there's not time today.

If there's not time today, don't kid yourself: there won't be time tomorrow, either.

Don't Sort Your To-Do List

The first thing to remember about setting priorities is that it does not mean sorting your to-do list. Just because something is on the list or on your schedule doesn't make it important. And don't assume that all the important stuff is on the list or your calendar already. I'll say it again: if you were already getting to all the important stuff you wouldn't be here, right?

Whether it's the tasks for the day or the major projects to implement, the core of setting priorities is deciding what's important—not what's easy or inexpensive. While cost and effort play a role, if you're not doing what's the next important thing, something's wrong.

Sure; there are exceptions. If you have a three-day project, and a five-minute task, knock out the task first. Just be sure it's really not the iceberg tip of a two-day task that should have come after the three-day project. If the project is going to require a loan or some time saving up funding but the task is purely a matter of time and effort, take that into account.

But don't decide what to do next *just* because it's easy or because you can afford it.

First Things First

An adjunct to that is in the word itself. 'Prior' means something comes before something else. Stop and consider whether the results of one project or task will affect what goes into the next one. Which makes more sense: getting more customers, or increasing customer satisfaction? Why not stabilize what you've got before trying to bring in more?

Big Things First

There's a visual analogy I love to use: take a small container (about a gallon) and put in as many tennis balls as you can fit. Now, pour in enough sand to fill the container.

Pour it all out into another container, and pour just the sand into the original container. Now, try to fit the tennis balls in.

You can't.

Same volume of contents, but it won't fit when you do the little stuff first.

The same principle becomes evident if you're creating something out of clay or toy blocks. It makes no sense to start with the details. You have to make the big parts before you can fuss with the little fiddly bits. Without the big parts, who knows where the little bits even go?

On Time, Low Cost, Top Quality: Pick Two?

Every project has three elements you need to balance: a deadline, cost, and scope, that is, the amount and details of the work to be done. If any one changes, at least one of the others must change as well. No matter how hard you try, you cannot do the same work in the same time at a lower cost, just by wanting it.

If you realize you can't allocate all the funds necessary to the project, you have two choices: change the deadline, or reduce the scope. If the deadline moves up, you'll either need to spend more money or, again, reduce scope. If the scope changes to include other elements, you'll be increasing the budget or moving the deadline.

With any project the solution will be individualized. Sometimes an element isn't flexible; your budget or deadline is fixed. In that case, your options are limited—which essentially means your decision is easier. The project may be more difficult, but if you had a fixed budget and deadline and you're not going to achieve them unless you reduce the scope, there's the solution: reduce the scope.

Understanding the triangular relationship of these three elements helps keep projects from running away from you (or running away with you.)

Don't Wait for Perfect

During the improvement phase of the DMAIC concepts I talked about under 'Planning', it's important not to try to be perfect. While you're setting priorities, don't waste time trying to find the perfect solution. It's much better to have a solution, but know it'll need adjusting, than to hope for the perfect solution which never materializes.

If you roll out a new program and then discover a flaw, fix it. You would have had to fix it to achieve a perfect roll-out anyway. This way, you've got something real and tangible to work with.

Time and Motion Economy

Some of the changes you'll make in your business operations will be attempts to increase efficiency. Streamlining is vital for small businesses (of course, it's vital for big business, too, but it seems to take decades for them to crash to earth; inefficient solopreneurs rarely even get off the ground.)

The next section will cover the time management matrix in detail, explaining how to use this perception tool to prioritize tasks and projects. But first, a quick note about process efficiency.

Most small business operators wear many hats. Spend a few hours doing this; a half-day doing that. Especially when a task requires some setup time (physically or mentally) you sometimes find yourself trying to get some economy of scale by sticking with the task long enough to make sense of the setup time.

How long do you have to stick to get those benefits?

Michael George, in "Lean Six Sigma for Service" states that the benefit of staying on one task before moving on to the next falls off rapidly after 10 times setup. In other words, if it takes 10 minutes to get ready for a new task, the efficiency of continuing on that task only lasts about 100 minutes, just over an hour and a half.

Measure how long it takes, physically and mentally, to set up for these recurring repetitive tasks. After 10 times that, give yourself permission to move on to something else if you want. You'll be fresher mentally and will lose almost no efficiency.

Time Management Matrix

Stephen R. Covey's "7 Habits of Highly Effective People" introduced a matrix to help with setting priorities.

To get the full benefit, please get the book and read all the accompanying information. It's one of the books you should have in your arsenal of business reading anyway; this is just one of many reasons.

Here's a summary of the time management matrix to whet your interest:

All activities in your business are either important or not; urgent or not. Gut reaction might tell you to spend time doing the intersection of urgent and important. That's wrong.

If you're focused on what's both important and urgent, you're living in crisis management. Fighting fires all the time will burn you out.

I hope it's obvious that activities which are neither urgent nor important shouldn't even be among your priorities. Those which are urgent but not important, the interruptions and things which seem important to someone else, can leave you feeling victimized and out of control. You're trying to get your work done and get stuck catering to others' whims.

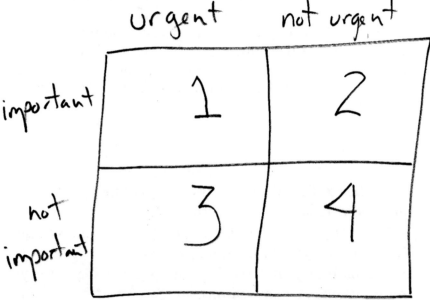

The solution to both problems, the burnout of quadrant one (urgent and important) and the interruptions of quadrant three (urgent but not important) is to spend as much time as possible in quadrant two, doing things which are important, but not urgent.

Quadrant Two

When something is important but not urgent, you get to implement it on your own schedule. No putting out fires, no delays due to interruptions.

These activities are where you're preventing fires instead of fighting them. You're planning, prioritizing, preparing. You're building relationships, not because you need something from someone (that's just a way of creating quadrant three problems for them) but because you see value in them, and have value to share with them.

These important but not urgent activities include recreation. Yup; that's right. This is where recreation fits in. Read the word differently: re-creation. Recreation, done right, is how you regenerate your desire to keep doing the stuff of life. (Done wrong, in the frantic fit-in-as-much-wild-life-as-possible manner many choose, tends strongly toward quadrant four: wasted time.)

This is another chance to get on your bicycle instead of running beside it. Invariably when planning of this nature is discussed someone objects that there's not time; there's too much to do already. That's quadrant one thinking and it's why so many of the hard-working people you know are facing the sad stress of burnout. Time spent in quadrant two is like payments against the principle on a loan. The time putting out fires in quadrants one and three is just making payments on the interest. Quadrant four is where you're burning money instead of making payments with it.

If you waste five minutes every time you do some task, in one year of normal business days you've lost more than twenty hours. If it takes you two hours to implement a change today, you'll start earning free time next month. Every time you pause to get on your bike instead of running beside it, you add two extra days to your year.

Make five changes and take a vacation!

A System for Getting Things Done

I said I wasn't going to spend too much time on nuts and bolts, but there is a system I've found which has really worked for me and I want to share it with you. It's specially designed for those of us who just can't seem to get organized and stay that way. If you find yourself forgetting important tasks, rushing at the last minute, putting out fires instead of planning in advance, this is a great tool.

Pam Young and Peggy Jones, authors of "Sidetracked Home Executives", created a program using simple 3x5 index cards to get control of their homemaking lives. I've used the basic concepts constantly for both business and personal activities ever since I read the book 30 years ago. Once again, this is only an overview; you'll get much more from the system if you read the accompanying material in the book. Besides, it's pretty funny.

Setting up a system like this falls into quadrant two; stopping to get onto your bicycle instead of running beside it.

The core of the system is a set of 3x5 cards and a tickler file with places for 12 months, 31 days and the 26 letters of the alphabet. Here are the steps:

1. Make a list of tasks you do on a regular basis. Oops; I mean, *should* do on a regular basis. Remember at each step that this system is about your goals, not your current habits. 'Regular basis' means any frequency, whether it's daily or yearly.

2. Give each task a time estimate. No; change that. Give each task a measured timing. You'd be amazed, once the system is in place, how much difference it makes

knowing that walking to the mailbox takes three minutes, not ten (or the other way around.)

3. Create a 3x5 card with the following information on it:
   a. Task
   b. Frequency; how often it should be done
   c. Duration; how long it will take
   d. Delegation: yes or no, and to whom; include instructions if necessary
4. Create daily, weekly, monthly and annual schedules for those task frequencies.
5. File each card you've created on the date (for this month) or month (for the future) it should be done.
6. Here's the hard part: end and begin every day with a look at the file cards. At the close of business, check tomorrow's cards to plan ahead. At the start of business, use the cards to plan the day.
7. As each card is completed file it in the day or month it's next due.

There are lots of details this overview doesn't cover, but I think even this summary will let you see whether a system like this can help you personally.

Performing

It's been said that dreams are great, but then you have to wake up and do something. Derek Sivers of the wildly successful CDBaby.com shares his thoughts on dreams versus waking up:

"It's so funny when I hear people being so protective of ideas. (People who want me to sign an NDA to tell me the simplest idea.) To me, ideas are worth nothing unless executed. They are just a multiplier. Execution is worth millions. Explanation:

```
Idea                          Execution
Awful = -1     multiplied     None = $1
Weak = 1       by             Weak = $1000
So-so = 5                     So-so = $10,000
Good = 10                     Good = $100,000
Great = 15                    Great = $1,000,000
Brilliant = 20               Brilliant = $10,000,000
```

To make a business, you need to multiply the two. The most brilliant idea, with no execution, is worth $20. The most brilliant idea takes great execution to be worth $20,000,000. That's why I don't want to hear people's ideas. I'm not interested until I see their execution."— *Derek Sivers, president and programmer, CD Baby and HostBaby*

You may feel that you'll get around to this or that eventually; that issues or problems will still be there when you're ready to deal with them, so what's the rush? Well, remember that in the absence of positive effort, weeds naturally grow. Every day we plant nothing we're growing more weeds. What one thing could you start doing every day, every week, however often, which would make a difference? Start planting flowers instead of weeds sooner rather than later.

Efficient with Machines, Effective with People

Efficiency applies to things. You cannot be efficient with people. You can't schedule in people like you do a conference room or some equipment or an event. Genuinely accomplishing things with people can't necessarily be put on a clock or a calendar.

With people, you have to be effective. While 'efficient' stresses streamlining, avoiding waste, shortest-path thinking, 'effective' points at the source, the power to produce a result.

We always want people to be efficient, to use what we see as the shortest path to the outcome. The problem is that, for them, it may not be the shortest path.

If you've ever seen electrical circuitry in a building, you'll realize that it doesn't always run in straight lines. Taking the time and effort to streamline the path of the wires just doesn't make sense when the materials are inexpensive, labor isn't, and electricity is really really fast.

When you turn on a light you don't worry about how the electricity gets there, as long as it does.

Instead of choosing the best path for the electricity, give people a desired outcome ('light is on') and let them make their own path.

Do Something!

There's a trick I play on myself when there's a household project I just don't seem to get around to. Right now, while I'm thinking of it, I go get one thing I'm going to need: the hammer, or the colored pens, a roll of string. I put it on the way from here to where I'll be doing the task, where I'll see it every day.

Next time I think of the task and I've got a few minutes, I think "Hey, the string's already right here; just go tie that thing and cross it off your list!" It's not a sure thing, but it helps immensely. Getting something in front of your face helps the results seem as real as the task.

The Journey of a Thousand Miles

When you're just starting, the outcome is a dream and the tasks to get there can be overwhelming. At the very least, they're huge compared to the imaginary outcome. Getting something real toward the outcome changes that balance enormously. (I'm sure it has something to do with the fact that you can't divide by zero, or zero times anything is zero; there's a psychological zero there somewhere.)

Remember how I talked about making vague plans first, and refining them as you go? The information you need to perform that refining comes from doing something. Take this first step, learn something, adjust the plan. Lather, rinse, repeat. Working in short loops helps keep the plan real and the goal flexible but realistic.

Short steps are easier to take. Small jobs get done; big jobs get planned to death. Another Joel (Spolsky) made the point in a presentation regarding software development that the longer a task takes, the less precisely you can define the time it will take. He recommended time estimates in power-of-two hours: 1/4 hour, 1/2, 1, 2, 4, 8, 16, with no task planned to last over two days. Longer than that, break it into smaller steps.

(Okay, here's a math thing, just because we're here: powers of two mean how many times you multiply two times itself. For instance, two to the second power, called two squared, is two times two, or four. Two to the third power, two cubed, is two times two times two, or eight. Two to the negative two power is one quarter. Unless you're planning on taking calculus I'm not going to explain that. If you really want the answer write and ask.)

Give Away Power to Maximize Power

True delegation results in an enormous increase in power, just like using a lever does in physics.

The average manager keeps the power balanced between themselves and what they perceive is the ability of their employee or even customer to manage things. With the fulcrum of power balanced between you, one unit of effort produces one unit of results.

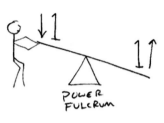

What if you moved the power closer to those who were actually doing the work? Give employees greater freedom to make decisions, to implement change, to interact with suspects, prospects and clients. And give those suspects, prospects and clients more power to determine their own destiny when doing business with you.

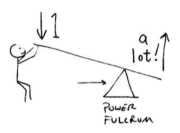

Moving the fulcrum of power closer to the work allows you to invest one unit of effort and create multiple units of results. Trusting employees to know what they're doing, trusting customers to interact in good faith, gives you a lever to increase your power while giving it away.

This doesn't mean telling someone else every step to take, then trusting them to take it. That's just management by remote control, and it's even more work than doing it yourself. If you've hired the right people, trust them. If you're interacting with the right suspects, prospects and clients, trust them. If you can't, your hiring or marketing systems aren't working, and until they're adjusted you'll have a hard time realizing the benefits of moving the fulcrum of power closer to the work.

Asking for Help is Always an Option

You're probably in business because you knew what you wanted to do and how to do it.

The downside is that the feeling of control that comes from doing it all is addictive. And before long, like any addiction, it's deceptive and damaging.

Unless you're Leonardo da Vinci, you have to ask yourself if you're really the best qualified person for every single task. Even if you really are (let's humour ourselves for a moment) is it really the best use of your time to do everything?

Where it's really dangerous is when, in a fit of confidence, we try to go it alone when we're really not qualified. The Do-It-Yourself habit becomes so ingrained that it's easy to forget to ask for help from someone more qualified. Then, it's hard to ask once you do remember.

Don't wait until you have no other options to ask for help. Asking for help is one of your options.

Use online forums. Build relationships with other VAs. Then when you need some help, you'll already have resources to turn to. I've developed relationships with several VAs, both in person and on the forums. I've several times needed a resource or some assistance and they've gladly given it. I've been able to do the same for others. Let's help and encourage one another. Let's not think we have to hold all the secrets to ourselves; sharing knowledge doesn't give us a smaller piece of the pie, it makes the pie bigger.

Successful business owners hire professionals to do those things that are beyond them. A grocer doesn't do his own taxes. He hires a tax accountant. A virtual assistant that specializes in marketing and has no accounting experience will also hire a tax accountant.

Focus on what you're good at and hire someone to do the things you aren't good at—whether it be bookkeeping, taxes, or marketing. Find your insurance agent, tax accountant, attorney and business coach before you open for business.

"In addition to scouring the latest and greatest in tools VAs use to provide services, it's just as important to incorporate areas like brand development, financial literacy, operational systems and hiring the best "team" (accountants, coaches, attorneys, insurance agents, anyone else who can help!)"
—Rachel Rasmussen, Rescue Desk, LLC

Professional Development and Education

A successful virtual assistant realizes that professional development is ongoing. Making sure you have reliable equipment or learning how to use the newest collaboration tools is only part of the picture.

A few things you can do to continuing educating yourself are:

- Take advantage of the many, often free, online workshops and seminars
- Buy business and marketing books at library book sales
- Subscribe to blogs and newsletters related to your niche
- Participate in online virtual assistant forums

Here's something not to do: learn a new skill just because you think clients will want it. If there's a new skill you'd like to have, that's wonderful. Eventually you'll add more value to your clients.

Eventually.

Right now, you'll be a newbie at bookkeeping or teleseminars or whatever your new skill is. You'll be competing, or perceived to be competing, with other VAs who've been offering their expertise in that area for a long time.

Since they're already experts, why not take advantage of their skills? Consider: if another VA asked you to help with a project, and made it clear that they respected your expertise, wouldn't you be eager to help out? You get paid to do something at which you excel; their client is delighted, and knows who you are now, and the VA who brought you in has enhanced their own professional appearance by sharing yours. Everyone wins. No one loses. Honest; no one loses.

On the other hand, if you already have a specialty, promote it! Be a specialist, not a generalist, if you can. There will always be room for generalists who excel, but if you're the best at something, the most passionate about it, you have an edge.

We're currently mentoring Annette Aiwohi of Emerald Spirit VA. Besides her administrative abilities, Annette is an excellent photographer. While photography isn't a virtual service, it *is* something Annette can offer her local clients to differentiate herself. It's something about which she's passionate. She doesn't need training to get started. Annette's tagline is apropos: "Our passion helps you focus on yours." Rather than learning a new skill and offering junior level help, she's sharing a passion. Sure, it's not directly related to administrative skills—which is exactly why it adds so much niche value.

What's your passion? What do you already know? Rather than struggling to acquire a new skill, ponder how you can use what you already know in order to stand out; to offer what marketing folks call your USP—a Unique Selling Proposition.

A Place for Everything and Everything in its Place

(Did you notice there's no apostrophe in that subheading?)

How many times have you found yourself at someone else's desk, in a temporary office, or some space where the work was familiar but the surroundings weren't your own? Organization can make or break efficiency.

If the space is neat and tidy, you can find whatever you need more quickly. If it's physically clean, not only is it more pleasant and hygienic but you're psychologically more likely to keep it tidy. In six sigma efficiency circles, they talk about the five S system:

· sort—eliminate what's not really needed
· straighten—arrange and identify with filing, labels, etc.
· shine—physical cleanliness
· standardize—create companywide standards (even if there are only two of you)
· sustain—make it a habit

Some systems add a sixth S, safety. Never ever sacrifice safety for what seems like efficiency.

Every task you perform, every project you undertake will be easier if you have a place for everything and everything in its place when it's not in use.

Chapter Four: Marketing

Getting things done is often broken up by business and project management types into three parts: strategic, tactical, and operational. Basically, that means deciding what to do, sorting out how to do it, and getting it done.

While I don't subscribe to rigid divisions of labor (I think anyone who doesn't grasp the tactical level is hopeless at strategy, and any tactician who doesn't know operations is doomed) for the sake of discussion it's helpful to isolate some concepts by which section they relate to. Make no mistake: as a small business operator or front-line manager, you have to be good at all three.

I've talked quite a bit about operational and tactical stuff; I'll be spending more time there in future chapters. This chapter will attempt to stick to broader concepts to help with the 'deciding what to do' stuff.

We're all marketing, all the time. We pitch our ideas to others constantly. We share the music we like, restaurant recommendations, books we've read. Humans are gregarious by nature. We spend our entire lives influencing and being influenced.

That's not a bad thing. Isn't it great when a friend, knowing what we like, connects us to some new music or points us toward a great hole-in-the-wall restaurant we wouldn't have found on our own? Believe it or not, that was advertising. Advertising is only a portion of marketing but it's probably the most misunderstood.

In those recommendations from friends lie the secret of marketing: when we hear a message we're interested in from someone we have a relationship with, it has value. We appreciate it, and hope it continues.

But picture advertising the way it's done most often: television, radio, and newspaper ads; what marketing guru Seth Godin calls "interruption marketing." You're watching a good mystery, and suddenly, it's interrupted with a pitch to have your car tuned up or the latest weight-loss gimmick.

Imagine the same tactics in our friends' recommendations above. There you are, discussing how much you love Mexican food, and suddenly they raise their voice to make sure you're listening and start telling you how great their car runs since they visited MagicTune. *You should try it! Here's their phone number. Call now to make an appointment!*

Does that really make you want to try MagicTune? And next time you want to chat about food, is this the friend you're going to look up?

This section on marketing will talk a little about advertising, but I'll stick mostly to the 'why to', and spend less time on the 'how to.' But first, let's address the part that keeps us from using a broadcast net to catch a single fish: the 'who to.'

Who To

Use a Pole, Not a Net

For a very long time the common thinking about advertising was (and perhaps still is) to spread your message as widely as possible, and those who are interested will respond. Untargeted marketing is, and probably always has been, an inefficient method; like using a net to catch a single fish. A properly baited hook will do the trick with less wasted time and effort.

The first thing a fisherman has to decide is what kind of fish they want to catch. Sure, maybe he doesn't care if it's bluegill or bass, but to some degree, you have to choose. If you're looking for catfish you'll make entirely different decisions about location and method than if you're interested in some yellowfin tuna.

What kind of fish are you trying to catch? Just anyone? Wrong. Unless you're selling something used with equal frequency and enthusiasm by everyone on the planet, that's wrong.

Try again. Remember all that stuff about trying for 100%, even if it's not achievable? Do that now. Describe your perfect customer.

Here's mine: I'm looking for an entrepreneur who's just starting out. They're creating a service business where they'll have lots of direct interaction with their clientele. They'll be in the market for one or two employees pretty soon, maybe even right away. They know their stuff, but they've never run a business before. Coming from the corporate world, they have lots of misconceptions about how things are done; mis-training about meetings, deadlines, budgets, chain of command; all the stuff that makes the corporate world so un-fun. Oh; and they've got some money to invest in start-up costs, so they see my services as an investment, not an expense.

I don't have a single client who fits that profile perfectly. They all deviate just a little. But just like goals let you know if you're making progress or when you've succeeded, creating the persona of your perfect client lets you compare each prospect or suspect with that persona and see if they are indeed a good client for you.

Don't just make this a mental exercise. Discuss it with your partners, employees, mentors. Write it down. Make this a real person, so that when they walk in or call, you'll all recognize that this is the one, your perfect customer. Until then, at least you'll have a good reference you can all share to analyze each suspect and prospect.

You may be thinking that your client can be anybody. This is one of the biggest mistakes you can make. It's important to narrow your focus so your prospects can find you and you can find your target audience.

When someone asks, "What can you do for me?", and you reply, "Anything", your prospect is not sure whether or not you can help them because your reply does not identify who you can help or what you can do. You need to give specifics on what you do, who you do it for, and how you can help that individual. Then your prospect will know whether or not you can help them and who to refer to you.

Create a detailed description of your ideal client. Be very specific. List specific skills you have and focus on those you really enjoy. This will help you clearly identify your target audience and the niche you will create for your business.

Creating a niche does not mean you cannot offer other services. It does mean you and your prospects will have a clear idea of what services you do offer.

Birds of a Feather, Part I

Aesop's aphorism applies in business, too. Sure, your vendors have an effect on the personality of your venture, but so do your clients.

If you've spent any time in business, you've had (or heard about) the nightmare clients who always want the best price, fastest service, highest quality—and then complain the whole time.

Would you be friends with someone like that? After a while, you couldn't help but become a little cynical and bitter, short-tempered and cranky.

What makes you think they're not creating the same mood in your business?

Make no mistake, you will become like your clients. You cannot change them, you can only choose the ones which don't need changing because they're already like you.

Reinforce your professional image by the people you sell to. Since it's all about relationships, why not make them worth having?

I Want You as My Customer!

Later I'll discuss how to approach your whole marketing and advertising plan. Right now we're discussing the 'who to' part so I'd like to address developing your advertising from that perspective.

Now that you've got a clear profile of your perfect client, ask yourself what advertising they'd respond to. Know, from an emotional perspective, what will move them, what will create a connection that compels them to contact you.

Be black and white; wishy-washy doesn't sell. Don't try to take the middle road. This is no time for compromise. Speak directly to your perfect client's passions. State strong opinions. Be yourself, but be an extreme version. If your message would annoy or alienate someone who's not going to be your client anyway, well, you can't lose what you never had. Your perfect client, though, is going to revel in your passion.

There's a brew pub near here where everyone loves to hang out. The food is pretty good, the beers are excellent, and the service isn't bad.

The music, on the other hand, is horrific.

Well, sometimes. Other times it's great. The thing is, one minute they're playing an obscure song by The Sweet, and the next they're playing something I can't stand. Next, something bland and boring, then an overplayed top 40 tune. Finally, back to something I actually enjoy, a straight country song, then off again through another round of this, that, and the other thing.

By trying to please everyone, they're annoying the people who care the most about the music. Anyone who can ignore the endless change train could ignore it as well if they just played one style of music the whole time. At least if I knew that for the next hour it would be music I can ignore, I'd ignore it. But the constant teasing of occasional interest is maddening.

There is no 'one size fits all'; that's only 'our size fits none.' Make your advertising message one size and let it be worn by those it fits.

Interested Influential Indoctrinators

Those are the only people worth advertising to. If they're not interested, they're not going to listen. If they have no influence, you may have made one sale, but if no one listens to them they can't spread the word. If they're not indoctrinators, folks who love to share what they've heard, they won't spread the word even if others would listen.

Your job is to know who's really interested in what you have to say. There's a certain amount of trial and error here; we'll discuss that a little later. But you can reduce the error part by knowing who your perfect client is; they're most likely to be interested.

Influential—advertisers discovered long ago that this doesn't equal 'powerful' when they started advertising to children. The average child can get their parent to buy anything.

Who carries some weight in the industry you're targeting? My greatest challenge is getting small business operators to realize that they really will benefit from my services. The best way to do that is to partner with acknowledged experts like the local colleges, small business development centers, and Chambers of Commerce. These business advisors know that most small businesses fail, and that most of those failures could be prevented. They're influential with the folks who are my perfect clients. This makes it a no-brainer for me to provide free training through these groups; their endorsement is exactly the remedy for the small business operator's reluctance to engage a consultant.

They're also indoctrinators. They have a mandate, in most cases, to help small business. Address yourself to those who want to spread the word. For instance, if you bake wedding cakes, while you should certainly address a certain portion of your message to brides and their mothers, they have a fairly limited interest (and range of influence) when it comes to advocating your services. Wedding planners and venues, on the other hand, are asked for recommendations all the time. They'd love to have another talented professional to send referrals to.

Why You Want Fewer Customers

The net-to-catch-a-fish concept of advertising was based on the idea that talking to more people was the best way to make more sales. It may still work to some degree. Spammers seem to be getting some kind of return for the millions of emails they send out, or they probably wouldn't continue doing it.

Annoying millions to make a single sale is no way for you to do business, though. You don't have the luxury of being completely amoral the way spammers are.

It's a marketing truism that it's better to sell more to existing clients than working to get new clients. And yet, the advent of the web seemed to make businesses forget that lesson. Everyone was focusing on getting as much traffic as possible, regardless of the quality of that traffic or the potential for conversion—actually making a sale.

Let's do some simple math here (yeah, it's gonna keep coming up.)

Let's say you have a conversion rate of 2%. That means that for every 100 people you pitch your services to, two of them become clients.

You've decided you need to do better than that; in fact, you want to double that. You could talk to twice as many people, 200, and now your 2% conversion rate nets you four clients.

But you had to convince 100 more people to listen to you. That's a lot of investment in emotional bank accounts; a lot of time planting flowers and waiting for them to grow, a lot of time cultivating interest.

How about focusing on your conversion rate? What if you invested all that planting and cultivating in the 98 folks who didn't become customers? If you can persuade just two of them, you've doubled the number of clients—by persuading, not 100 people, but 2.

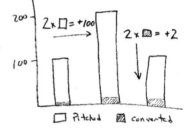

Don't do fifty times as much work if you don't have to.

Here's another benefit for the start-up business: if you're depending on having 1,000 customers to succeed, you've got a lot more work ahead of you than if you only need 100 customers to succeed.

More Golden Rule

When you're creating the persona of your perfect customer, remember, this isn't you. While your clientele will probably share many of your interests and traits, don't make the mistake of misapplying the Golden Rule. I may love Rocky Road, but you may like vanilla, or maybe you don't like ice cream at all (perish the thought.)

If I'm committed to selling Rocky Road, I'm sunk. If, instead, I'm trying to create a pleasant after-dinner atmosphere for you to enjoy, my options are much broader. And that's what the Golden Rule is about: when I want a little snack, I want what I like. So do you. It doesn't have to be the same thing.

You're not me, and in the end, that's a good thing. Don't assume your clients are you.

This realization can also help you avoid offering products or services which are doomed from the start. In our dessert scenario, I suspect that if your apple pie was only available with cheddar cheese melted on it you'd have a hard time selling it. I'd eat it; it's delicious. But being from Wisconsin makes me a little funny about cheese.

When I was in Ireland, some pubs carried quite a few beers on tap, but all had at least two: there was always the traditional Guinness, and there was always Bud Light.

Bud Light? In Ireland? Yup; according to every publican we spoke to (in horrified hushed tones) all the younger generation prefers fizzy American lager. The older folks and some tourists like the dark stout, so they keep that around, but they sell what customers want, not just what the publican likes.

There's a balance to be found there in any business, but don't fall into the trap of assuming that the Golden Rule means that everyone is just like you, liking your likes and disliking the rest. Good listening skills and genuine interest in others comes into play once again in doing this market research.

Cutting Edge & Perfection Can Be Your Enemy

Being first to market is every innovator's dream. Unfortunately, most of the brilliant ideas are already taken, and the ones which aren't just may be beyond our reach to implement.

Being the best in the world is important; there's no point marketing yourself as 'a pretty good consultant' or making your tagline "As good as the next guy." But 'the world' can be a smaller place than, well, the whole world. In fact, it had better be. It used to be that your 'world' was the local village, the local neighborhood. If you were the only bread store, book store, blacksmith, or doctor in the village or neighborhood, you were, by default, the best.

The internet has created the perception that our world is a much bigger place. You may not really be competing with a bread store across the world or a doctor in another country, and you'd better not be trying to compete with Amazon.com, but that perception is there. Trying to be the best in **that** world is an exercise in futility.

This is another place refining the vision of your perfect customer comes in handy. Know what their world is. Pitching yourself to too broad a spectrum makes it that much harder to be the best in that world.

Maybe there's already a guitar shop in town where they do repairs and setup. Make a smaller world: become the local expert on electric basses. Refer guitar work to the other guys, and focus entirely on a smaller world to be the best in. Before long it will become known that you don't work on guitars, only basses. Where am I going to take my Fender P-bass, to the generalists or the specialist? You're now the best in the world, by making a smaller world to be best in.

Being the best in the world, though, isn't purely about quality, trying to achieve perfection. Sometimes perfection is a waste of time.

I recently read an article in a music magazine where the writer wondered if people are ready for the 'lower quality recordings coming out of home studios' and being sold online these days.

Ready for it? People are clamoring for cheap music. As far as I've been able to tell in my 45 years of listening (I'm not counting the years when I couldn't speak yet) I've come to the conclusion that the average listener couldn't care less about quality recording, or, in fact, about quality performance. They care about snappy tunes that touch them emotionally, which they can hum later and sing along with after a few listens.

It's a classic mistake musicians make: garage bands playing clubs will invariably include long blazing guitar solos, at least one drum solo, some fancy bass work—hey, let's show off our musicianship.

Nobody cares.

Nobody but other musicians, and they're 1) a smaller demographic than 'everyone' and 2) usually in the lower ranges of your economic target (what's the difference between a guitar player and a medium pizza? The medium pizza can feed a family of four.)

So, if you're obsessing about quality on your recordings, unless you're recording exclusively for other musicians, you're wasting your time. No, I'm not saying you shouldn't care. Just applying some Voltaire something-or-other about good enough versus perfect.

Be the best in the world. Just be careful how you define 'best' and 'world' and you'll do fine.

Why To

It might seem obvious that the reason for marketing is to generate business. Exactly what 'generating business' means might be less obvious.

If your only goal in your advertising message is to make a sale right now, you're just a salesman. Do you like it when someone is obviously and overtly selling to you? Neither do I.

You should be marketing all the time but that doesn't mean being a salesman all the time. We'll talk later about how marketing is like dating and marriage. To prepare for that, let's talk (again) about how people think and why knowing that lets you speak so they'll listen to your message.

Every virtual assistant just getting started wants to know how to market to get new clients. We'll touch on some basics in this book. There are many, many books about marketing. I encourage you to read everything Seth Godin, marketing guru, has written - his books and his blogs.

Marketing takes time and the successful marketing strategies today are different than they were a few years ago. Successful strategies include networking and referrals which are covered in the next section.

Plan to market your business every day - post a blog entry, use Twitter, make a follow up call, send out a postcard.

Start a blog and set up Google alerts for blogs in your industry. Comment on industry-related blogs.

"As a virtual business owner it is imperative that you have a website at the very least and be familiar with the latest technology trends."

—Lee Drozak, My Office Assistant

Networking and Referrals

It's been my experience that the majority of my clients come from networking events and referrals. For that reason I encourage you to attend networking events at least twice a month. Your local chamber may have mixers you can attend as a guest. Join Meetup.com and find local events in your area that relate to your niche.

You may wonder just how effective it is to attend a networking event to get new clients. Here's my success story. In August 2007 I accompanied my husband, Joel, as his guest to a Meetup group for web designers since my husband was trying to promote his web business. In September one of the members of that group signed a contract for my bookkeeping services.

In November of that same year I accompanied Joel to the Sacramento Speaker's Networking Meetup as his guest. I have attended those meetings every month for over a year and now, in addition to being an assistant organizer of the group, have nine clients that I met directly at those meetings and another seven that were referred to me by those clients. My prospect list includes an additional seven people that were referred by members of that group. Yes, networking does work!

Word of mouth referrals are the best way to get clients. The trust and relationship you have built with your client transfers to the person they refer to you. When that referral contacts you, they already feel they know you to some extent.

Recently the power of word of mouth referrals really hit home for me. One of my clients told one of his business partners about my services. The business partner and I communicated by phone and email. Before we could arrange a signed contract, he had already referred my services to several other people. In fact, one of his referrals signed a contract for my services before he did!

Social Networking

"Everything I have read states this is an important aspect of your business, however it fails to explain how you go about doing the networking."

—Jessica Nix

Some find social networking intimidating. They wonder how to connect with others and what to say. This is a constantly evolving tool and much has been written on social networking.

The major social networks are Facebook and LinkedIn. There are others specific to virtual assistants such as FindVirtual.com and Virtual Assistant Forums.

Tips on Using LinkedIn:
- Spend 15 minutes on LinkedIn twice a week
- Make sure your profile is complete
- Recommend others
- Ask for recommendations
- Update your status twice a week; include a link to your blog or some other useful resource once in a while
- Use all the new applications available: upload your WordPress blog; add books you are reading to the Amazon application, create an event, etc.
- Join appropriate groups and start and add to discussions
- Ask and answer questions

It can be overwhelming trying to keep up with all the social networking. For that reason I strongly encourage you to pick two or three and have a meaningful participation on each of those each week. The more active you are on a social networking site, the more people will get to know you and the more likely you are to make good connections and eventually find new clients.

If you spread yourself too thin by trying to be on every social networking site there is, you'll wear yourself out and not develop the kinds of meaningful relationships with others on the site you need to succeed.

As with everything else you do, schedule regular time each week to spend at your social networking sites.

Peacock Feathers

Another age-old (mostly) false belief about advertising is that just 'getting your name out there' has some kind of value. You know better. Remember that witty, funny, or surprising commercial you saw on TV last night, or heard on the radio this morning? Who was it advertising? Chances are you have no idea. Being clever does not, in itself, guarantee meaningful delivery of your message.

That doesn't mean name recognition has no value, it just means it has limited value. What the marketing folks refer to as 'signaling strategies' can have real impact if you do it right.

Signaling strategies are like a peacock's tail feathers. They don't add value to the bird; the don't make it stronger or tastier or a better provider for its family.

However, the bird which is strong and a better provider probably has the best tail feathers, and the hens know it. So, while the feathers don't add intrinsic value, they signal intrinsic value while creating enormous emotional appeal.

Signaling strategies are more likely to have the desired impact if they're actions rather than words. Instead of just talking about your successes, celebrate them publicly. Just landed a really big client? Throw a party and invite, not just the new client and your existing clients, but your suspects and prospects as well. Make it lavish. Make a big splashy impression about how excited you are about your clients.

Not only will people remember it and talk about it, because of its personal nature (they were there in person) they'll remember who gave the party. Your name will be linked with the signal, not lost behind it as so often happens with witty commercials.

Consider ways to flash your peacock feathers to those suspects and prospects you'd most like to bring into the harem. Remember, who you choose as clients reflects who your company will become. Incorporating some quality DNA is worth a little time, effort and expense.

I Don't See What You're Saying

Communication is the art of getting the picture that's in your mind into my mind. Unless I get essentially the same picture, we haven't communicated no matter how much has been said.

Words are notoriously bad for communicating; there's that old saying about how many words a picture is worth. The average person isn't very good at envisioning what you're talking about. Get used to using visual aids as much as possible, and if you can actually show people what you do and how you do it, so much the better.

People Don't Buy What They Need, They Buy What They Want

Okay, of course people buy what they need, but when they do, the first consideration is usually price. If we have to buy it, at least we'll get the best deal.

We're not like that with wants. When you were planning your last vacation, buying that new dress, or selecting a gift for a loved one, cost probably wasn't the prime consideration. We want what we want; we're worth it, whatever it costs.

It's so easy to slip into the 'need' mindset with our customers. We're so excited about our service that we can't imagine their life without it. They need it, right? We just unwittingly made cost their prime consideration.

If they really need what we're offering, they'd have it already. That doesn't lessen our value, it increases it: what you're offering really is brand new, special, and unique. Help them see how useful, attractive, easy, fun it is, and let them want it.

People will buy what they want.

If You Can't Be Number One, Be the New Number One

Back when we talked about persuasion we agreed that you can't persuade someone your baby is the cutest by telling them that their baby is ugly.

This applies to getting folks to switch products or services, too. Since we make decisions emotionally, we're usually pretty personally invested in the choices we've made. Convincing someone to abandon a decision they've made means convincing them they were wrong; essentially, that their baby isn't the cutest.

At the same time, you're fighting against whoever is already first in the market. A statistical concept called Zipf's Law says, essentially, that first choice, the most common item in any group, doesn't just edge out second choice. Instead, first choice is likely to be twice as popular or common as second, second twice as common as third, and so on. A little math shows that if you're further down the chain, your share is 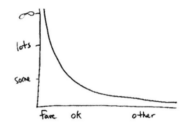 microscopic. Right now we're convincing someone to change their mind, despite the fact that they've already made a decision (either to use a competitor's product or service, or none at all.)

If they've already made a decision, that's their baby. Telling them they were wrong isn't an option. Much like Napoleon's pontonniers, instead of telling them they're going the wrong way, offer to build them a bridge. Give them, instead of a replacement for what they've already got or another version of something they don't want, a brand new idea. Once again, be the best in the world—in a brand new world.

Adding the Free Prize

Seth Godin's fantastic book 'Free Prize Inside: The Next Big Marketing Idea' talks about what marketers call 'soft innovations' which are, in essence, the free prize. The basic psychology goes like this: when Lincoln-Mercury started putting expensive Bose stereos in their cars, they discovered that half of their buyers opted to have the $8,000 stereo added to their $12,000 car.

If you're not an audiophile, that probably doesn't make much sense to you. Do you have kids? Do they eat breakfast cereal? Have you ever tried to buy a cereal that didn't have a free prize inside?

They couldn't care less what the cereal tastes like; they want the prize.

Seth makes a few interesting points about creating soft innovations:

- people want the free prize more than the thing itself; for instance, Lincoln-Mercury discovered that some people were buying stereos with wheels, not cars
- the prize satisfies a want which is often totally unrelated to the purchase, rather than delivering more of whatever is being bought
- saving money doesn't count; that's psychologically a need, not a want

So, here's the concept: add something really cool but **totally unrelated** to your service. Make it spectacular, **even if you have to charge extra** like Lincoln did with the Bose stereos (you don't think they threw them in free, did you?)

Years ago, in another housing bust, a home in San Diego wasn't selling. The owner re-ran the ad, mentioning prominently that it now came with a brand new Porsche in the garage. It sold immediately, despite the fact that the price of the house had been raised even more than the cost of the car. When you're playing this game (we're talking about wants here, so let's call a spade a spade) money is not the issue.

- Offer your gardening clients a new, deluxe service. Let them know they'll love being home so much, you're including a catered dinner the first month.

· Bring a massage therapist into your waiting room, and give everyone a free massage while they wait for the doctor, the mechanic, whoever.

· Give a pricey Amazon.com gift certificate to your best coffee shop customer every month.

Notice that the free prize, while not directly related to your product or service, isn't totally random. Folks who have a professional gardener probably enjoy their home and would like the luxury of a special evening enjoying it. Folks who are waiting probably need a good chair massage more than most of us. And regular coffee shop visitors are likely to be either music lovers or book lovers, or both.

Selling a want is way better than selling a need. If you include an exciting free prize, you can sell that as the want.

Getting a Foot in the Door

Tricky salespeople and political speakers know the trick of getting people saying 'yes' quickly and often. There's an ethical way to use this as marketing research.

Research has shown that people who agree to a small commitment are much more likely to agree to a subsequent greatly increased commitment. On the other hand, when approached directly with the greater commitment the success rate was closer to 5%.

This isn't a way to trick people into making the greater commitment, but a way to investigate whether or not it's even worth pursuing. It confirms the concept that it's better to increase sales to an existing customer (the greater commitment) than continually seeking new customers.

If you're attempting to persuade, it works better to start with the thin end of the wedge. Get people behaving differently in small ways and they're more likely to make a big leap when it's called for.

Lack of Loyalty in the Workplace: The Good News & the Bad News

When my father was young, it was common for a man to find a job right out of school and keep it the rest of his life. He changed careers more than once, but once he'd settled into production and quality control for electronics, he stayed with the same company until they laid him off around the time he turned 50. He worked as a consultant after that, but I don't think he ever understood how a company could show such a lack of loyalty.

I've changed careers more than once, but even within the computer industry, I've managed to change jobs about every three years. That's not an uncommon statistic these days. And the fact that the last two 'changes' were caused by the company I worked for going out of business isn't uncommon, either.

Some companies still do business the old way: they're the mother hen/big brother, and you'll do what they say, partly because it's in your best interest, and partly because they said it. They're still operating as if the brief period of one-way loyalty that caught my father off guard still existed: employees will do as they're told because the company is boss.

Businesses no longer have power over employees and clients. It doesn't work to tell the customer to *take it or leave it; that's all we're offering; look right here in the contract, we don't owe you a thing.*

You're no longer just competing against the one other business in town. You're competing against the prospect's perception that they can get anything they want from anywhere in the world on the internet. You're competing with the employee's perception that anyone can start a web business, selling on eBay or building websites.

Whether those perceptions are true or not (they're not) isn't up to you. This 'free agent' mentality leaves the door wide open for you to amaze and surprise your employees, and your suspects, prospects, and clients with loyalty. Treat them all as if you'll always be there for them; that they're a partner, not just a source of income. Of course, you really have to mean it, but you're a new world entrepreneur—sincerity is an intrinsic part of your makeup, right?

How To

Promise Big; Overdeliver

That's the three-word course on marketing. If you truly get that you can skip the rest of this section. If you'd like more detail, read on.

Much of the practical how-to stuff in this section is culled from the writings of Seth Godin, and from an excellent free book from 37 Signals called 'Getting Real' which, while primarily about software development, promotes an unconventional but practical perspective on project management which I've adopted as part of my marketing method.

Abstract is Out

As I've mentioned often, people don't have vision. They don't read the fine print or look under the hood (or if they do, they really don't know what they're looking at.) Most folks think they saw what they think they saw and don't bother with the rest.

When it comes to telling these distracted busy people about yourself, you can't be abstract. They need to be able to create an immediately recognizable mental image of your unique selling proposition.

CD Baby uses this concept when new bands set up their accounts by asking, who do you sound like? Instead of using vague abstractions like 'lilting witty alternative country rock' I can tell you that my music sounds like Roger Miller, Chris Isaak and Bob Dylan meeting at Johnny Cash's house.

When you're working on the persuasion aspect, it works to tell folks who you're not instead of who you are. Position yourself as someone's opposite in some clear manner. For instance, I'm not a business coach. Coaches don't play; they're on the sidelines, shouting encouragement. Coaches give instructions, usually through a bullhorn. Coaches replace team members, mess with the roster, and leave (or get replaced) when the team is failing.

Nope; I'm not a business coach. Instead, I'm a business mentor. A mentor's goal is to help you find your own answers. They don't give instructions, they help you figure out what to do. They don't make decision, they guide you to your own decisions. A mentor feels a personal investment in your success; by its nature, mentoring necessitates genuine emotional involvement.

Now, if I'd written all that about a mentor without prefacing it with why I don't use the term 'coach' it wouldn't have nearly the same meaning.

Be someone's opposite. Feel free to base your message on what you're not, if it helps define who you are.

Bam!

Do you like baby food? Why not? Bland. No spices, no sugar, no salt. No intensity.

So many marketing pitches are as bland as strained squash. Trying once again to reach everyone and avoid alienating anyone, businesses create messages which manage to say as little as possible in a quiet, apologetic voice.

If you're going to appeal to your perfect client, you need to be tasty; you need intensity. The spice in your message is your passion, your strongly stated opinion. Be yourself, of course, but an amplified, more intense version. Be black and white. Make strong assertions. Wishy-washy is strained squash. Be passionate or be quiet.

A little side note: did you know you don't taste spices? Your taste buds can experience sweet, sour, salty, and bitter. What we call 'spicy' is when a food activates *pain sensors* in your mouth. Some folks even get addicted to the burn of spicy foods. So don't worry if your marketing might be a little intense. The folks who don't like it wouldn't necessarily change their minds just because you toned it down, and the folks who do like it just might become addicted to your brand of spice.

Nobody Wants Boring

People buy what they want. 'Needs' can be boring. Doesn't matter; you need them. But nobody buys a boring want.

I hope you're passionate, exuberant about what you're selling. I hope you really believe you're the best in the world, because you can't fake passion, and you can't sell boring.

When your passion connects with your perfect client, you'll have more than a sale, you'll have an advocate, a spokesperson. 'Remarkable' has two meanings: the one that means amazing, and the one that means worth talking about. If you make it the former, it'll be the latter.

Shout your message. Amuse and occasionally annoy with your intensity.

While you're working on being the best in the world, invest some thought in what Seth Godin calls 'edgecraft.' It's right in line with the idea that you don't want to call yourself 'as good as the next guy', you want to call yourself something intense and unique.

Forget comparatives, the '*-er*' words. Find a superlative (an '*-est*' word) that tells an intense truth about you and your business. But it can't be vague generalities. You need measurable empirical data which supports your claim to an edge.

Tell Me a Story

Another way to avoid boring is storytelling. A list of facts, however useful, is boring. A story which illustrates those facts is memorable and emotional. Chip and Dan Heath cover the subject in their book 'Made to Stick' where they explain how to tell a simple unexpected concrete credible emotional story.

I used to buy as much of my clothing as I could at Banana Republic, back in the old days. I loved the story told by the catalogs and stores about people traveling the world, gathering tough and unusual army surplus gear for me to wear. I didn't care if it was true, I cared if the clothing was as fun as the story.

Once they were bought by a large corporation who changed the image from a story to a store, I stopped buying. I can get jeans and shirts cheaper elsewhere. I can't get a story anywhere but where it's told.

Every business has stories. This is a place to be an extreme version of yourself. Be yourself; authenticity is critical because people have zero tolerance for fraud. But when someone spins a good yarn, we don't worry so much about whether the details are perfectly accurate; it's a story, and we know it.

I tell stories about my dad in my business. They're all fairly accurate, based on things he really said and did and taught me. I'll bet, though, I couldn't prove any of them.

Here's a good touchstone for the stories you tell (verbally or visually) about your business: if someone knew the unvarnished facts, would they be angry or upset, or would they smile knowingly and enjoy being an insider?

A good story behind your product or service makes it better. It makes the user feel good about their choice, it makes it easier to share it with others.

A good story involves superlatives, edgecraft. It tells a unique tale about you and your business, something the listener can't get anywhere else.

Try a Bite

Giving something away is a classic technique to generate interest. It's also an excellent way to weed out the disinterested.

As you're walking the aisles of the warehouse store trying the pickled beef or marinara fish sauce, you know instantly whether or not you like it. There is absolutely no better way for a prospect to decide to use your product or service than to experience it first-hand. There's also no better way to determine that they're not designed to be your client.

The movie industry has it right. Long before a movie comes out, you start seeing ultra-brief teasers at the theater and on television. As the release gets closer, you see longer previews. Anticipation is cultivated regularly until the release, when the excitement generated by the teasers and advertising can outweigh the actual quality of the movie.

Give something away. It doesn't have to be the whole enchilada; create an edited version, a sample size or shorter plan. But make it the real thing, with real value. Letting folks look but not touch doesn't work. Giving away another copy of your sales pitch is useless or worse, even if you label it a white paper or research document.

If you are going to promote through education, do it right. If you're a professional, the expert, create something that'll help your prospects and suspects even if they choose to do business elsewhere. Now you're reinforcing your professional status while making a deposit in your emotional bank account with them at the same time.

Educating Prospects and Suspects

"I found the most challenging obstacle for me when networking during chamber events or meeting potential clients was the need to educate the public on what a Virtual Assistant is and what we can do for them."
—Michel Randolph

Most prospects tell me they aren't sure what a virtual assistant does or how they can best utilize our services. It can be very challenging to explain what it is we do. If we have a niche, it can be easier to describe exactly what it is you do.

My website also offers a list of 30 projects that a virtual assistant can accomplish within an hour. This list has given prospects a better idea of the types of things we can do for them. One prospect had read that list and saw I offered transcription services. She hadn't been aware of that and this was something she needed. So now we're working together to do that.

This year I am using two questions to help prospects determine how they can best use my services:

1. What are the things you do that don't increase your energy? We all do things we really enjoy and that energize us. We also do things that tend to drain our energy. Those are the things I want to know about so I can help you with them.

2. What are the things you do that don't directly increase your profits? You know - those tasks that have to be done in a business but don't directly bring in income. Again, those are the things I can help you with.

I also offer a free report when someone signs up for my monthly newsletter. This report includes information a business owner can use to determine how to find the right virtual assistant and other valuable information designed to educate business persons about the virtual assistant industry.

The Four Rules of Advertising (Don't Stop After Number Three!)

If you've read anything by Seth Godin, you've read that powerful advertising is personal, anticipated, and relevant. This absolutely eliminates interruption marketing. It eliminates mass mailings to random addresses. It eliminates traditional radio and television advertising.

Within the parameters of personal, anticipated, and relevant, here are the rules:

1. Persistence—People probably aren't looking at or listening to your ad as they're about to make a buying decision. Be the name at the top of their mind.

2. Regularity—If you're their top-of-mind choice, it's nice to know your ad will be coming around again soon. Persistence and regularity work together to create the general awareness most folks associate with advertising.

3. Clarity—One ad, one message. Make it obvious what you're selling, who you're selling to, when it's available, where to get it, and why they should buy it. Yeah, the five newspaper Ws.

4. Testing and Measurement—This is the one advertisers hope you forget about. They don't want you to know how miserably most advertising fails. Make sure every single ad you ever run has some unique identifier (phone number or extension, email address, web address, etc.) which will tell you (without asking the customer; it's not their job) which ad caught their interest. Run your original ad a few times, regularly, in the same place. Then, once you've tabulated the results, change one thing.

Change the headline, or the photo, or the day. But change only one thing. Run the ad the same number of times you ran the original, and compare the results. If the new ad is less effective, change it back; if it's more effective, keep it. Make another change, but only one. Test some more. Lather, rinse, repeat.

Advertising without testing makes no sense. Institutional or image advertising simply reinforces the single least important level of permission advertising, brand trust. It's hard to build and easy to damage. We'll come back to that in a bit.

Marketing is Like Dating

Dating with a view to marriage, that is. It's a long slow process involving the other party's interest and participation. Chasing a single transaction is no way to start a marriage, and it's no way to create a viable business relationship.

Your first challenge is to be interesting. We'll assume that what you're selling has value, or you'd be doing something else. So, you're interesting.

Your next challenge is to decide who you're interested in. You wouldn't settle for just anyone to marry; why settle for just anyone to share a business relationship with?

Next, you have to find someone who matches your interests. Some folks write personal ads; some look around at work; some hang out in singles bars or online singles groups. The quality of the result is often tied to the level of effort you invest. The same is true in your search for your target market. If you just buy a mailing list, assuming it's full of your perfect clients, your minimal effort will return minimal results. Building a database of truly meaningful contacts over time will create a smaller group of much better quality results.

Okay, so now you've found someone you're interested in. Now you have to make them interested in you. This is where all the stuff we discussed earlier about persuasion comes in. You can't win an argument, you can't persuade by telling someone they're wrong or pointing out that their baby is ugly but yours is cute. You can't change their mind. The only reality is their perception. This is the long, slow grind to actually making a sale, and there's no quick fix, any more than you can force someone to be interested in marrying you. And, in that same manner, some suspects or prospects who looked good on the surface turn out to be the wrong choice. Say goodbye with good grace and move on.

Now that you've got some great prospects who seem to be interested, spend some time with them. Increase your investment of time and effort, and at the same time, work toward increased permission to speak to them. You want the relationship to become more intimate as time goes by.

In the end, you want them to stop thinking of you and themselves separately, and start seeing the two of you together. You want them to see your business as their partner, not just a store or salesman who sells them things.

Congratulations; you're married. If you continue investing time and effort in this relationship, no one else will be able to entice this client away because they'll be just as invested in the relationship as you are. You can't get that from a mailing list.

Be aware of other similarities to marriage. For instance, the permission you've gained in this relationship isn't transferable. Just because you get to hold their hand does not mean you can take food off their plate, or that they'll magically want to watch football or figure skating with you. If you've gotten permission to discuss your XYZ Service with them, you do not have permission to talk to them about totally unrelated services or products. That has to be earned separately, although the existing relationship makes that easier than starting from scratch.

This permission is also non-transferable to other parties. You're the one who's married, right? Your permission to speak to the client does not give you the right to give their contact information to someone else, any more than your marriage implies permission for all your friends to hold your beloved's hand.

Also be aware of one big difference: in a marriage, we'll hope neither party has complete control. In your new business relationship, that's not true. The customer has absolute control. The instant they lose interest or trust, they can end the relationship without a word to you. It's not a one-time victory; it's a battle you have to fight every day to keep them loyal because they do not owe it to you.

Talking to Friends is Better Than Talking to Strangers

A friend, embarking on her first entrepreneurial voyage, asked about direct marketing letters. It drove home the point that every single dollar my company has earned has come from word of mouth.

While it's unusual to hit 100%, in line with 'marketing is like dating,' I suspect that most of your qualified customers knew who you were before they ever spoke to you. Talking to friends is easier and more productive than talking to strangers.

Share your story, your passion, your hopes and dreams with people who know you—and to whatever degree, care about you—and they'll pass it on to others. That way, everyone who hears about you, hears it from someone they know. And that makes you a better risk than a complete stranger, by some groovy exponential amount.

Before you spend time talking to strangers about your business, make real sure everyone you already know is aware. When you do start talking to strangers, get an introduction; find some way to be a friend of a friend, rather than a stranger. People don't like giving money to strangers, but they'll do business with their good ol' boy network 'til the cows come home.

Levels of Permission

As described in 'Permission Marketing' there are five levels of permission. From your least control to your greatest control, they are:

1. Situation—Someone happens across you when they need what you have; this is just being at the right place at the right time. The fact that you have no control doesn't make it bad, just unpredictable. Being prepared will help you nail this opportunity almost every time, though. People love convenience; if you're convenient, they'll love you, too.

2. Brand trust—This is the traditional name recognition; permission based on who you are. This is hard to build and easy to lose. Although you have some small control, unlike situational permission, this is the least valuable level of controllable permission.

3. Personal relationships—If someone trusts you, you have greater permission than a stranger.

Relationships tend to be one-to-one, though, so this type of permission doesn't grow. Because it's personal, it's easier to hang on to. The other party feels invested in you and is less likely to wander.

4. Points—This is an incremental rewards system. (Yes, I'm going to explain what on earth that means.) When people feel like they've joined your party, you have greater permission to speak to them and sell to them. There are two versions of this:

a) Points—Remember S&H Green Stamps? Think about the little punch card at the coffee shop, where you buy 10 items and get one free. For each purchase made, the buyer gets a little something toward a benefit. Each little bit has value toward the final result, sort of like earning money to buy something, except it's only good for buying from you. This can be fun, but it can be a lot of work.

b) Chance—Here, each purchase earns the buyer a chance at something free, usually something bigger than that earned by the points model. This works for four reasons:

   i. People who bother to enter a contest tend to be optimists; they enter because they think they'll win.

   ii. Once they're invested because they've got three or five or fifteen chances to win, they'll keep playing. No one quits when they think they're winning.

   iii. Folks will invest time and effort into playing the game because they see it as effort toward the prize. They'll give you their attention, which they might not do otherwise.

   iv. Contests are fun. How often do people get to have fun while they're doing business?

Creation and Innovation

Coming up with new products or services may seem less of an ongoing process than marketing said products or services. That's true, but less true than you think.

Ever notice how, when your favorite sports team is on top, management starts messing with the line-up, making changes and generally driving you nuts? Why would they do that?

They do that because they know the cyclic nature of success. Nothing lasts forever; your product's or service's success will spike when it's new and exciting, dip as you grow and build it, then climb to a shiny new bigger peak.

And then, it will drop off the other side. Into another dip.

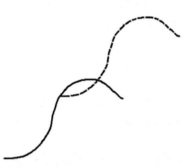

The way through that second dip is to use the upward momentum you've already got to start something new, so that the initial dip on this new thing is already higher than the initial dip on the previous thing. Stairsteps of spikes and dips, but always trending upward, along with your fame and fortune (or whatever your personal business goals are.)

See that gap where the curves overlap? That's the chaos of change. Success makes change even more scary, and even more important.

This section is tied closely with earlier thoughts on how people think, because creating a successful product or service depends heavily on those concepts.

It's Not About You

If you're just selling something, you're a salesman. Nobody's going to come hunt you up to sell them something. But solve a problem, and things change. Folks will go to great lengths to find a solution to their problem, and if you've got that solution they'll want it, and they won't be too fussy about what it costs.

Name your product or service for the problem it solves, not the technical process you used to create it. When you describe it, don't talk about how it works, talk about how it helps. Keep that focus on the customer and what it does for them, because frankly, they don't care about the details that interest you. They want to know what's in it for them. Remember that the greatest unfilled emotional need is to feel special and important. Show them that you've got their best interests at heart by making it clear that you're solving a very real problem for them.

Marketing in Thirds

It's easy to make the mistake of offering two choices, one absolutely tip-top, with a price to match, and one dirt cheap, that's, shall we say, lesser in quality? But when you're marketing a 'want', that's dead wrong.

Most people, when faced with a decision like that, have a 'default' setting; the easy choice. And, as you might guess, humans tend to be economical creatures. Offer a third choice: better quality than the least expensive, less expensive than the top-of-the-line model.

Now, people can reward themselves, showing their discerning taste, without being extravagant. Well, that's how they'll rationalize it; in the end, virtually all our decisions are made on emotion and rationalized afterwards, but that's another story.

It also works if only the middle choice is you; the others can be your competitors, Ms. Top O'TheLine and Mr. Economy Model.

Being the Best in the World in a Smaller World

There's an old story about two hikers who run across a bear. Surprised, they turn and run with the bear in hot pursuit. One breathlessly says to the other "I don't think we can outrun this bear" to which the other replies "I don't have to outrun the bear, I only have to outrun you."

You do not have to be the first to market with a new idea. (Note: there are no new ideas. There just aren't. Don't burn a lot of mental cycles trying to be completely original.) In the thought-provoking 'In Search of Excellence' Tom Peters and Bob Waterman discuss a number of companies which achieved excellence by being second to market. By allowing others to make the tough decisions, to implement the ideas that didn't work, by feeling out what the market wants, they were able to focus on tried and true solutions.

They had to do it excellently, of course. You can't be second in quality if you're second to market. You now face the challenge of differentiation; making it clear that you're not the other guy.

This also applies to complexity. Some problems are easy, and some are hard. If you have what it takes to achieve a goal like curing cancer, I think you have a moral obligation to do so. Most of us, though, are looking for a better way to clip our toenails or for snacks that aren't filled with sugar or salt or fat.

Especially if you're a neophyte in the world of business, work on simpler problems. Find a basic need and fill that. You probably don't have to look any farther than your own problems. Find something you really want fixed, find a solution, and market it.

Keep It Simple

Remember when we talked about things which complicate decision-making? One of the biggest culprits is too many choices.

Don't make things complicated. Simplicity wins over complexity every single time. A simple product or service is easier to explain, and easier for prospects and suspects to grasp.

Simplicity also nudges you toward a more defined target market. It helps you to avoid trying to be all things to everyone, which is a losing proposition, sort of like the music that's played in many public spaces like the brewpub I mentioned earlier.

One way to actively implement simplicity is to find out what folks don't want. Find something they could do without, like the 'Cancel' button I hate on my toaster.

Strive for a zero training requirement. Ideally, what you're offering should be simple enough that it doesn't require a manual or training to realize a benefit. All other things being equal, folks will choose understandable over confusing.

More Tries Equals More Successes

With some things, better aim and careful planning lead to the greatest success. When you're dealing with what's untried, untested, and dependent on the vagaries of human feelings, there's a big element of gambling. If you're trying to roll doubles, trying harder doesn't help; rolling more often does.

When scientists are analyzing genetic changes, they use fruit flies, not elephants. Not only is small easier, the fruit flies have a much shorter generation span. Faster turnaround on your marketing experiments means faster learning. More rolls. More successes.

They're Not Mistakes, They're Learning Opportunities

In the same way that complaining customers are like an engine noise that can help you find a problem and fix it, 'failed' marketing experiments can point you toward what's broken. Often, when something works, it's hard to say why. When something doesn't, you've got a better chance of discovering why it didn't.

Sherlock Holmes said (okay, so it was really Sir Arthur Conan Doyle) that once you've eliminated the impossible, whatever is left, however unlikely, is the solution.

Use the test/fail/learn/repeat cycle to help you eliminate impossible marketing challenges. Some products or services or approaches are never going to work because of inherent flaws you never would have seen in your mind's eye. Getting them into a real-world situation can bring those flaws to light and allow you to eliminate them, working toward what's left, however improbable.

Your Greatest Challenge

I've mentioned before that fear is a powerful motivating factor. Your greatest challenge in creating and marketing your product or services is overcoming fear.

Doing something new is scary. Change makes people uncomfortable. Try this: fold your hands. Notice which thumb is on top. Switch thumbs. Feels awkward and uncomfortable, doesn't it? Now imagine a change that actually **means** something. Scary.

We have an innate desire to be seen as special and important. What we don't want is to be seen as *different*. We still want to fit in. We all worry that standing out means standing alone.

Edgecraft is hard, not because it's hard to imagine some new extreme to introduce into our service or the free prize associated with it. Edgecraft is hard because we're comfortable in the middle, not at the edges.

The problem is that being in the middle isn't remarkable, and doesn't get you noticed. Being edgy is scary, but remarkable.

Chapter Five:
Operations Strategy

Why To

Another opportunity to experience the benefits of unconventional thinking is in the actual operation of your business—deciding what to do and how to do it, but especially, why to do it.

Most small businesses are stuck in the century-old Frederick Taylor time-and-motion-study headspace of 'getting things done.' The apparently logical reasoning is that streamlining and efficiency are empirical concepts requiring lots of measuring and cutting. Draw lines, and keep clear what's inside and what's outside. Make rules and enforce them strictly. Keep order. Managers manage and laborers labor. (Corollary: laborers do as they're told or they're replaced.) Create economies of scale because bigger is better.

While that may have been the way to function in the early days of the industrial revolution, today it's a recipe for disaster. Remember earlier when I complained about compromise, where we each give something up in order to do business together? Here's that same negative concept. Ruthless rationality tends to be exclusionary. It leaves out serendipity, passion, and the vicissitudes of fortune.

Usually Bee, but Sometimes Fly

A number of business books (In Search of Excellence, Strategy Bites Back, Strategy Safari) refer to an experiment reported by Gordon Siu. Try this at home! (Don't get stung. Maybe just try it in your head.)

Place six bees and six flies in a clear glass bottle and cover the end with your thumb. Lay it on its side on a window-sill, so all the little flying creatures can see the sun through the base of the bottle (you're doing this in the daytime, right? If not, wait 10 to 12 hours and try again.) Take your thumb off the neck of the bottle and leave it open.

Bees outsmart flies exponentially. The smart little bees bang against the bottom of the bottle, trying to fly to the brightest light they can see. Glass is an unfathomable mystery to them. They bang and bang and bump—until they die.

Flies are pretty dumb. If flies have a brain it's never been found. To them, glass is also an unfathomable mystery, but so is the rest of the physical universe. The dumb little flies bang against the glass *wherever they happen to be*, completely ignoring that bright shiny object through the base of the bottle. They bump and bang and flit around (as flies are wont to do) and, eventually, through sheer flailing, they happen on the neck of the bottle and escape.

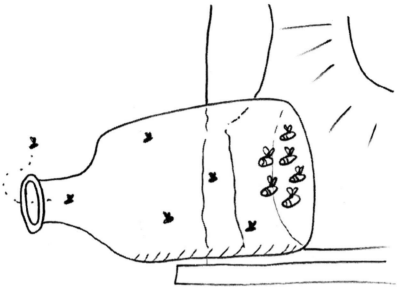

Here's the danger: we think we're smart. Even if we're humble as pie, we still think we're pretty smart because that's how humans operate. No matter how smart we are, the universe is more complicated (or much simpler) than we imagine. Eventually, we'll encounter circumstances where flying toward the brightest light, the most obvious solution, will lead to absolute failure, because we fail to prepare for an unfathomable mystery.

Being overly rational favors ideas and actions which match what we're already doing. It tends to reduce experimentation, seeing failure as a bad thing instead of an opportunity to learn.

Often, the bees will be right, and the brightest light is the right goal. Once in a while, though, the random but relentless fly will succeed.

By Your Bootstraps

"The Bootstrapper's Bible" by Seth Godin is essential reading for those of you who are considering self-employment or this whole entrepreneurial thing. It's excellent reading for any business person.

In it, he describes the five things big established businesses have that you don't: access to money, a distribution network, a known brand, existing customers and employees. Then, he describes the seven things you have that they don't:

1. Nothing to lose—When you're just starting out, if you do it right, you can consider everything expendable; an experiment.

2. You can be happy with the small fish—In fact, you can be a small fish. Instead of being a shark, looking for big prey, and lots of it, you can be a remora, the little fish that swims beside the shark eating the scraps that are too little for him to care about.

3. Direct presidential input and access—Your customers can go where the buck stops, right at the top. And you get to have a direct say in everything that does on, which lets you finely craft your business in its developmental stages.

4. Rapid research and development—Depending on how much caffeine you have access to, ideas can become reality in a much shorter time because you're the entire team. Failures can be learned from and scrapped without filing endless reports or wasting time in face-saving justification attempts.

5. Perception as the underdog—You're David, going up against all those Goliaths. Everyone wants you to win, because somewhere along the line the big guy has cheesed them off, and you (hopefully) haven't.

Everyone cheers for the little guy, the 'every man' going against the corporate behemoth.

6. Low overhead—This means lower costs to you, not necessarily to your clientele. It's a huge supporter of item #1. If you haven't tied yourself to an expensive long-term lease on office space because you can work in your attic, basement, or dining room, you've got less to lose. Sometimes that means you can negotiate pricing with prospects, but let's try to develop a less price-sensitive marketing plan.

7. Time—You're not racing a deadline, you're simply working toward goals. You're below the radar, so spending a little more time on the test/fail/learn cycle or on your real life isn't as much of an issue if you were the CEO of a busy corporation. Slow, organic growth will let you nourish and prune as you go.

Be very aware of the advantages the big companies have and stay out of that competitive space. If you try to steal the giant's lunch, he'll eat you instead. But lean heavily on your advantages. Develop your operational strategy with them clearly in mind and you'll have a long, long lever to pry against any challenges.

Humility

Remember how being just a little bit smart caused trouble for the bees in the bottle? It took more than half my life to learn the practical value of humility (I'm still working on it, but at least I know why.)

Entrepreneurs are risk-takers, risk-embracers by nature. It requires a certain amount of hubris to take on the world like that. While you can never be completely prepared for the type of unfathomable mystery that glass is to a bee, being aware of your own limitations (or at least acting like it) can sometimes be the difference between sticking your neck out, or putting it on the chopping block.

Customer-Centric Thinking

When you're creating your operations strategy, ask yourself these questions *in this order:*
1. Is this the best thing for my customers?
2. Is this the best thing for my company?
3. Is this the best thing for me or other individuals involved?

Do what's right for the customer, first and foremost. Big things, small things, visible or invisible. They give you the privilege of being in business. Reward them, and they'll continue to give it. Put yourself first and they'll know it.

Cooperative vs. Individualist

Game theorists (and now business consultants) talk about a problem called Wolf's Dilemma. Imagine you and 19 casual acquaintances are in individual booths, invited there by a wealthy eccentric. All you can see in the closed booth is a large button. You're told that if you all refrain from pressing the button for the time you're there, you'll each receive $4,000. However, if anyone presses the button, all pressers get $1,000 and non-pressers get nothing.

Do you press, and get a guaranteed $1,000 or do you hold back, hoping everyone else does the same?

No, really—which would you do?

We're naturally concerned about being left behind or left out. It's human nature that we want to protect ourselves; unselfishness is a learned trait, not an inborn one. What happens, then, is that when we're unsure of the other chap's intentions we tend to act selfishly, reflexively protecting ourselves. In the case above, if the stakes are altered so that if everyone refrains from pressing the button the reward is $10,000, or the payment if anyone presses is reduced to $100, it sways the results significantly.

In Wolf's Dilemma, it's clear that when the stakes aren't extreme, taking the risk of acting unselfishly yields greater gain. It's true in real life, too. But imagine another scene.

You find exactly the right domain name for your business, but someone else already has it. It seems, though, that they're not really using it, so you offer to buy it. After agreeing on a price, what do you do? Do you send money, then hope they actually do transfer control, or do they transfer control, trusting you to send the money?

In the cooperative version, you each get what you want at a fair price. Over and over again, I've seen the individualist version: nobody acts, because neither is willing to risk trusting the other. Of course, in this transaction, you can use a broker; someone who will, for a fee, act as middleman for the transaction. Of course now you have to trust them (they're probably bonded, so the risk is reduced) *and* you've paid extra just to avoid trusting a stranger.

In an ongoing relationship the risk reduces greatly with each transaction, but with both sides leaning toward the individualist reaction, an ongoing relationship is going to grow more slowly—if at all.

Eight Attributes of Excellence

It's no secret I'm a fan of Tom Peters, and his book with Bob Waterman "In Search of Excellence." I found it interesting that their list of eight attributes of an excellent company all require a certain amount of humility to implement.

1. A bias for action—Done right, this includes leaky systems; that is, everything is designed to allow someone with an idea enough latitude to appropriate finances, people, time, whatever they needed to experiment. The systems and rules are relaxed enough, leaky enough, to encourage experimentation without endless red tape.
2. Close to the customer—Customer first. Always.
3. Autonomy and entrepreneurship—Give employees, contractors, even customers the ability to make their own choices and be self-actuated requires getting ourselves out of the way.
4. Productivity through people—I'll be spending some time on hiring practices later, but once you've got people on board, trust them and get out of their way.
5. Hands on, value driven—The enormous concept of management by walking around; making sure the decision-makers know what the front line is doing and trust them to know the answers.
6. Stick to the knitting—As you grow, stick to what you do best. Creating new products or service outside

your area of expertise (usually because there's money in it, usually because it's the latest craze) is arrogant and dangerous.

7. Simple form; lean staff—Einstein's advice: make things as simple as possible, but not simpler. More on the 'lean staff' part when we talk about hiring and cultivating great employees.

8. Simultaneous loose/tight principles—Clear rules and guidelines (again, as simple as possible) but nearly absolute freedom within those simple boundaries.

Birds of a Feather, Part II

Everyone you have business transactions with helps define the personality of your business. Your own personality plays a large role, but don't underestimate that played by customers, vendors, peers and of course, employees.

Don't hire employees based entirely on their skillset. Don't trade with business peers based only on your financial or systemic needs. Don't choose vendors based only on price. And don't choose customers based solely on their ability to pay.

You can garner better quality customers by spending more than seems warranted for quality and service. Spend a little more to ensure that everything is the very best it should be. Spend the time and effort and money to provide world class service, promptly. Make it clear that you highly value your customers, and folks who appreciate that will want to be a part of it.

Embraceable Change

Know, from day one, that everything is going to change. Our nature conspires against us once again; we can go to great lengths to avoid change.

On top of the fear of change I've talked about before, there's also the challenge of allowing ourselves to change our minds. We come up with a brilliant idea and spend a little time with it, pondering it, maybe even doing something about it. That's fine so far. Just remember that your first idea isn't always your best idea. The longer you spend learning about a problem, the better you'll be able to resolve it. Sounds like a later idea might be a better idea. Having more ideas is easy, inevitable. The trick is to let go of the old ideas so the new and improved can slide in.

Even harder: someone else has a later idea; someone close to the problem, who's learned more about it. Here's the clincher: their new idea, their method of dealing with the current challenge, isn't demonstrably better than your original idea.

It takes a lot of humility to accept that someone else's idea might be better, especially if it's primarily better *for them*. Going back to the concept of autonomy, let the folks who are dealing directly with an issue determine the best solution. Unless they're violating the spirit of the business (in which case you should be educating them) the front line knows the answer.

Reduce obstacles to change. Don't require meetings or committees or paperwork to enact the right thing. Don't make folks jump through hoops to present their ideas. And for heaven's sake, don't make folks feel embarrassed or dumb or unappreciated when they have ideas.

Oh; and if you're not the final decision-maker, remember that while you may enlightened and humble, seeking the best solution regardless of whose it is, others may not have joined you in the new millennium. If you're on the front line, you know the solution to the problem. Unfortunately, there's just no connection between how good your idea is and how quickly or easily it will be accepted.

Change, Constant Change

Good sports coaches know the benefit of changing a winning team. When your momentum peaks, you're not just going to continue going up. The normal cycle is a falloff after that peak. Good coaches and business managers know to use that momentum to start something new. Make changes now instead of after the peak, when momentum is actually negative.

This isn't advocating change for change's sake, it's a way of working with the energy of natural cycles instead of fighting it.

Fearful Power

Fear is a powerful motivator. It's not a good one, but it's certainly powerful.

When I've performed music in the past with beginners who aren't used to being in front of a crowd, I've suggested the possibility that their body can't tell the difference between fear and excitement; that, perhaps, if they convince themselves that it's the latter and not the former, the increased pulse, fidgets, and sweaty brow are good things!

Stop for a minute and think about the one thing you really hope doesn't come up when you're talking to clients; the one thing you really hope isn't going to happen at work today.

If you can turn the source of your fear into an asset, you're now burning to talk about something unique to yourself, and eliminating the primary show-stopper from your own mind.

What's your greatest fear? Why isn't it an asset?

Simplicity

Plan for simplicity. There's a reason quick-moving athletes usually look so trim; agility goes with leanness, not bulk.

The more people involved in any decision, the longer it will take to make. Although we're not numbers, the math is interesting: between two people there is only one communication path. Among three, there are three. Add a fourth, and you've got six; a fifth, and you've got 10 (it keeps increasing in a series called triangular numbers; every individual you add increases the number of communication paths by the number of people who were already there.)

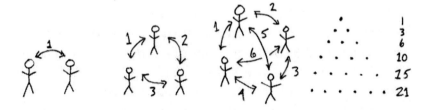

Any complications to the planning and preparation processes are unnecessary delays, costs, and frustrations.

That includes unnecessary paperwork, now, and forever. If anyone in your business is more interested in getting the forms filled in than in helping customers, find out why and change it.

Adaptability

Humility is a gentle quality, and it will help you embrace change gently. If you wait until you're backed into a corner, then react to change in a frenzy of activity, it's like the change that occurs when you blow a balloon up too far. Instead of driving in change with a hammer, gently nudge things toward what works. Maintaining a state of continuous small changes is more natural than fighting to maintain status quo, then reacting when there's nowhere else to go.

Businesses suffer entropy, the natural concept that everything tends toward disorder. Processes, left unchanged for years, or even just months, can be outdated before you know it. Going back to a concept from 'Getting Things Done', measure everything. Once you've got a system in place, the 'Control' part of implementation allows you to monitor the new process, and to know when it needs adjustment. Whether it's the Hawthorne effect or practical changes, anything you measure will improve.

There's another psychological danger here, though. We often see connections where there aren't any. Remember the tech support caller who mentioned that when they pressed the spacebar on their computer, the phone in the next cubicle rang, but only sometimes? Measuring helps keep improvements improved by taking things out of the realm of gut-level instinct and into a real connection between cause and effect.

Entrepreneurial Drive

The final point I'd like to make regarding the 'why to' portion of operation strategy is to shoot for the moon. Yes, perfection may be unattainable in real life, but if you're aiming for 100% and fall short by 10%, you still hit 90%. Aim for *that* as a goal and fall short by 10%, and even though the shortfall is 10% smaller in the second case, you've only hit 81%. I don't subscribe to the concept that if you don't like what you see you can always lower your standards.

Your passion is vital to your success. Don't sacrifice your real life, but your business needs your love. Talk about it. Look for opportunities to share your passion and others will pick it up and share it with others when the conversation turns that direction.

Passion lets you look at the big picture and the long haul instead of instant gratification. Passion makes you jump into the trench with a shovel when that's the right job. Passion makes you indignant at any shortfall or failure without personalizing it, alienating the real live human beings who people your business, inside and out.

How To

When you're planning any activity, humility is still hanging around. It's easy to decide what to do based on theoretical information. Theory needs a reality check.

- Is what you're trying to do physically possible? Something as simple as arranging furniture in the office can become a debacle if you don't check to see that those two desks really fit between the corner and the door. Back to some math we did earlier: the fact that it takes you 10 minutes to unload two large items from the delivery van does not mean you can unload 24 of them in two hours. You'll get tired. They have to go somewhere. Remember to account for reality.

· Is what you're planning doable by you and your team? Planning to build your own website doesn't make any sense if no one on the team has the necessary skills. List the skills necessary (and identify the black holes) before you commit to a project.

· Is it worth doing? Some projects are fun or sexy or high-profile. Those are occasionally good enough reasons to invest time, effort and money in them. Usually they're not. In the section on "Getting Things Done" we talked about identifying desired outcomes; knowing in a measurable way whether or not you've reached your goal. If you can't identify the desired outcome, try again. If you can, and the answer is not something that benefits your business, put it on the list with your hobbies.

This does not mean that if you don't have perfect circumstances you shouldn't attempt something. Constraints can be marvelously inspirational; look what happened to music when the 12-tone scale became the de facto standard for music in the Western world. This 'limitation' inspired one of the greatest surges of musical creativity and productivity in human history.

Constraints can be the genesis of some very creative thinking. Just remember to re-do the reality check on each new creative solution.

A few random thoughts:

· Maintaining open communications among your team, or with your mentor if you're working alone, is absolutely vital to good brainstorming. People have to know their ideas will be listened to and given appropriate attention, regardless of the speaker's position in the company.

· Develop an 'open source' mentality, not just with software (although that's a great cost-cutting place to start if you've got the right team.) In general, don't assume the expensive or brand name product or service is better. Don't scoff at do-it-yourself ideas from within the company; the fact that something was created in house instead of purchased has no bearing on its value to your company.

· Remind yourself in every strategic decision that it's about the customer. In the end, which software or how much you pay to rent the fancy store-front has much less to do with success than your passionate obsession with making every single customer feel like the center of your universe.

Mission Control (Vision, Too)

Your business needs a mission statement. It needs a vision statement, too.

Your vision statement should come first. This is the inward-looking part. What's your dream? How will you be more fulfilled, more fully expressed by your business? Where, in a high-level way, do you see yourself and your company in a few years?

Your mission statement is outward facing. Who are your customers? What do you do for them? How do you do it?

Now that you have a vision and mission statement, with the former on the wall where you can see it and the latter on your website and every other wall, where everyone can see it, revisit and rewrite them every six months, or every time there's a significant change in your business. Keeping them forever is like making your kid wear the same clothes to high school he was wearing when he was 12.

That being said, here are our vision and mission statements as of the exact moment we're writing this chapter:

Joel's Vision: I want to help small business operators to be happy in their work while still having a life outside of it; to help them earn enough money not to worry, and help them be recognized as good employers, quality vendors, and good citizens in their community because they focus on others instead of themselves.

Joel's Mission: I help small businesses build on the trust that comes from communication that's more human, and help create career renegades who make a great living doing what they love.

The Mission Statement of Awesome Assistant is: To partner with my clients, helping them save time and money by providing administrative and marketing support. Working together we create and implement strategies to promote their businesses. Values of sincere interest, reliability, high integrity and remarkable service motivate clients to refer my services to others.

Find a Mentor

Having to make all the decisions for your business can be wearing, physically and emotionally. Doing it when you enter uncharted waters can be paralyzing. A mentor, someone who's been there before, can help turn it into an adventure instead of a terror.

Don't confuse mentoring with the friends you have a drink with after work. While peer review can be helpful, you're looking for the single most qualified person you can find who's willing to offer specific guidance on specific challenges, and help with the reality check on your plans. This means someone you might think is out of your league. Don't aim too low, though. You'd be surprised how willing some of the very smartest folks are to offer their expertise, and how pleased they are to be recognized.

You're asking a big favor here. Make it easy for them to say 'no' if that's the right thing for them. At the same time, make them want to say 'yes' and do it sincerely. Make it clear how much you value their expertise. Show them how closely their business or personal philosophy aligns with your own. Let them know how easy you'll make it for them to help.

A few years down the road (or maybe sooner) remember to return the favor to the new kid on the block.

Use Freelancers

Not everyone loves the thrill of the chase, the buzz of taking a calculated risk and seeing it pay off, the adrenaline burn of knowing you have to make the tough calls. Some thoroughly talented folks who prefer not to be tied to an office 9 to 5 are self-employed, but not entrepreneurs.

Freelancers rent their skills to multiple bosses. If you need an accountant four hours a month, a freelancer is a godsend. They often work from their own office, sharing their time among a number of clients. They continue to hone their skills, staying on top of the latest stuff, garnering economies of scale by focusing on what they do best. You pay only for the exact skills you need, as often and as long as you need them.

Sue is a virtual office administrator. She does all kinds of administrative tasks from bookkeeping to typing to web work for a handful of clients. She's not their employee, she's self-employed. At the same time, she has the relative security of knowing that she's not responsible for their strategic implementation or personnel problems. She doesn't face any of the usual entrepreneurial challenges; her clients do all that for themselves. What she does is free them up to focus on what they do best.

A VA may need to hire freelancers. I've heard VAs saying they know nothing about accounting so want to learn it all so they can manage their own books and offer bookkeeping services. If that's not a skill you already have, plan on spending a long time and a lot of effort to get to the point that you're ready to offer it as a paid service. For your own business, if accounting isn't something you really have a burning desire to learn, why not hire a bookkeeper instead?

Chunk

Short deadlines are easier to reach than those far away. Small teams are easier to manage. Big problems become easier to solve if they can be broken into smaller chunks.

The small team working on the little problem with the short deadline will also do better if they're volunteers, if they set their own goals within established guidelines, and are only committed to this project, not permanently fused as a team.

Built-In Change

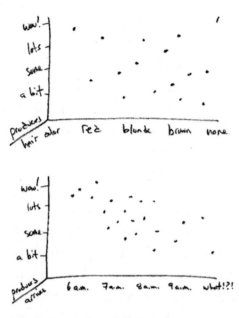

If you're starting a new process or monitoring a process you suspect is broken, create a system to give you feedback in short cycles. Don't wait a month or even a week to measure whether something changed. Use the shortest time frame that make sense for the process. The sooner you learn, the sooner you can change it and test it and monitor it some more.

Once your best minds have fine-tuned the process, though, get it out of their hands and into the hands of folks who excel at doing the same tasks the same way day in and day out. Let them assembly-line the new process, and get the innovative creative types working on the next improvement.

When you're analyzing, stick to the data. You can't go with your gut; if your gut knows the answer, how come the process is broken? Scatter plots are an excellent graphing tool to help see whether or not there's a relationship between two items. If it seems like an employee's starting time affects productivity, plot it; start time across the bottom and productivity up the side. If there's a relationship, the dots will be grouped along an imaginary line. The closer the relationship, the clearer the line will be. If the dots are scattered all over the place, you've just discovered a non-connection.

When considering a solution to a problem, don't just ask if Solution A is the right answer or not. You don't get world-class thinking that way. There should be multiple options so you can compare Solutions A, B, and C, and take what's best from each, synthesize a few concepts that fall between, and create Solution M or Q.

Chapter Six: Business Operations

Most of my tips on day-to-day business operations have been covered in the sections on "How We Think" and "Getting Things Done." This section will focus primarily on two aspects not yet covered: staffing and money management.

Do I Need a Business Plan?

A successful business owner needs to have a business plan. It doesn't have to be a 45-page document. In fact it can be as simple as one page. It just needs five simple paragraphs describing your vision, mission, objectives, strategies and action plans. You can learn more about the

One Page Business Plan® at their website and download sample plans and a template.

Kelly Harris, founder of FindVirtual.com, provides some questions to ask before creating your business plan:

1. *What skills will I offer? What am I currently proficient at? What have I have been hired to do in the past?*
2. *Who will my target audience be? Executives, Corporations, Small Businesses, Males, Females, Elephants...*
3. *Do I need a Web site? What do I want on it and who will do it for me?*
4. *What is my total budget for marketing, supplies, etc.?*
5. *What will I charge and will these charges be commiserate with the job description?*
6. *How will I organize my work day?*
7. *Do I want to do this alone or joint venture?*

"This is a living, breathing, growing document that spells out your mission, vision, niche, brand, pricing strategy, service offerings, sales projections, operational plan, marketing strategy, disaster recovery, expenses, capital and much, much more. Skip this step and it's like jumping into the ocean without a life jacket. You may stay afloat for a while, but eventually you'll sink"

—Rachel Rasmussen, Rescue Desk, LLC

Staffing

Why Hiring the Right People Matters

In a small business, you can't afford the luxury of a team of specialists. For many of us, the team is me, myself, and I. Even if you have a small handful of employees, they probably wear a bunch of different hats throughout the day.

The size of the team dictates two things: you have to hire excellent generalists, and they have to naturally and instinctively support and improve your company's personality.

It's Not About Mechanics

Here's a formula for writing a best-selling book: find a best-selling author, read everything they've written, and write something like that.

Even though that's exaggeratedly simplistic, can you imagine the results of even the most careful and studious attempt to write a novel this way? It's obvious that this isn't how a good book is written, how great music is composed or performed, how the great screen performances were created.

There's more to it than the mechanical skills. There is something innate in each of us which makes us excel naturally at some things and struggle hopelessly at others. And it's not about whether we're talented or not; everyone is talented—just not at everything. I've never read a great novel by Humphrey Bogart. Never heard any great music by P. G. Wodehouse. Don't expect to see Van Morrison in a great movie.

Skills, Knowledge, and Talent

I highly recommend Marcus Buckingham and Curt Coffman's "First, Break All the Rules" if you really want to understand what makes folks tick in a professional environment. One thing that resonated with me was their concept of 'talent' versus 'skills' and 'knowledge', concepts I'd arrived at long before I found their marvelous book.

Skills are the 'how to' stuff. My wife knows about bookkeeping. She knows touch typing. She can use word processing and spreadsheet software with ease. She knows how to bake a pie, how to drive a car (either kind of transmission.)

Skills can be taught. Each of those things can be broken down into steps to follow. You can learn word processing from a book or a website. You can bake an edible pie from reading a recipe in a book. No, you won't be great at either, which is where this is going.

Knowledge is what we're aware of mentally. You know the way to the store. You know (hopefully) whether or not you can jump over a puddle that wide. You know the password on your computer.

Some knowledge is factual: basic math, vocabulary, traffic laws and driving directions. Some knowledge is based on experience: you know not to run with sharp objects, when to cross the street and when to wait, which restaurant has the best pizza.

None of these things are talent. Bogie, Pelham, and Van all had skills and knowledge. But each of them had (or has) something else: their unique driving force and perspective on what matters and what doesn't, and their ability to apply that to what they were doing.

How Talent is Formed

Most of us think of sports, music, or movie stars when we hear the word 'talent'. That's only part of the story.

Each of us has ways of thinking and behaving which come naturally to us. We don't have to try; don't have to remember to do it. It's how we're wired.

And that, in a nutshell, is what talent is: how a person is wired.

At birth, we each have billions and billions of nerve cells in our brains. Each has thousands of connections to other nerve cells. During the first three years of life, we learn to walk and talk and develop our fundamental personality.

But then, it's too much. Our mind, the ethereal thing that exists in the spaces between the cells, starts pruning connections. It strengthens the ones we use the most, allowing others to atrophy.

Before we're out of our teens, some paths have transformed into superhighways where everything moves at the speed of light. Others have shrunk to jungle paths where every step requires slashing through the undergrowth. Although we can clear the paths through the jungle to some degree, after a certain point it seems that fundamental change, turning them into superhighways where traffic flows effortlessly, might not be possible.

Your talents, determined by those effortless paths, are the behaviours and thinking that happen naturally and automatically. Of course, to have business application, someone has to recognize the talent and have a practical use for it—but it's not like looking for the next Bogart unless you're casting a mystery movie.

Buckingham and Coffman dispense with two myths about talent:

1. Talents are rare and special—The truth is everyone has talent. It just has to be recognized and applied to the right role.

2. Some roles are so simple they don't require talent; anyone can do them—Having tried, unsuccessfully, to run a janitorial business, I know how wrong this is. I can clean my own house like nobody's business. My wife often comments that I've done a better job in the kitchen than she would have. I love being surrounded by cleanliness. But someone else's house or business? Not interested. No matter how much I charged, it just didn't matter to me whether their floors were sparkling clean and all the trash liners were replaced. It's not the cleaning I love, it's the clean. Excellence in any role requires a deep driving desire that's aligned with the core of that role.

They also define three kinds of talents: striving, thinking, and relating.

Striving talents are our motivations; why we do what we do. Some examples they give are:
- achiever: self-starters; an constant internal drive to be or do more
- mission: your beliefs just have to be put into action
- service: you feel compelled to be of service to others
    Thinking talents are our methodology, how we go about things. Some examples they give are:
- arranger: the ability to orchestrate (people, events, etc.)
- responsibility: the desire to assume personal accountability for your what's going on
- problem solving: the ability to find solutions despite incomplete data

And finally, relating talents are how we interact with others; our relationships:
- empathy: you can identify others' feelings and perspectives
- multi-relater: a networker
- stimulator: creates enthusiasm, drama

To get a good overall picture of talent in the workplace and how you can ferret it out in prospective employees and even yourself, I highly recommend spending some time with Buckingham and Coffman's writings.

Who to Hire

Whether you already have employees or have just reached the point that you're considering your first, don't fall victim to corporate thinking in your hiring practices.

Take a look at a résumé, any résumé. Beyond the victim's vital statistics, it lists facts they know, skills they have, and tasks they've performed—that is, if it's thorough.

Here's what's wrong with that: these things, in themselves, do not make a good employee. This is true in a large corporation, but it's life or death in a smaller business. The facts a person knows, the tasks they've performed in the past, the mechanical skills they have don't tell much, if anything, about what they're like as a person. They don't tell about their passions, their motivations, what makes them *them*—the talents we've been talking about.

So, coming full circle back to hiring for a small company: if every member of a small team is going to be wearing multiple hats, you're looking for people who love to learn and are easy to get along with. They can learn how to operate that piece of machinery. You can indoctrinate them into how **you** stock the shelves and convince them that your operating hours make sense. They can develop skills and gain knowledge. But you won't change their talents.

Good communicators learn faster and are easier to get along with. Someone you can converse with productively on a professional level, and enjoy chatting with on a personal level, has a good chance of being a good fit. People who are good at communicating (that includes speaking, listening, writing and reading) are almost always doing it naturally. They'll readily learn really core things like customer service and management skills.

The Opposite of Hiring

On the flip side, you may already have employees whose talents apparently aren't suited well to the role they're currently in. If you have a role they'd fit in, offer to move them. If you don't, you can still offer to move them, but in this case, it will have to be to another employer.

We're not talking about problem employees here; that comes in a minute. These are good folks who simply aren't in a role that lets them express their talents. Maybe you've got a guy who loves being the center of attention, great with people, but he's a lousy mechanic. If you can't use him at the front desk making customers happy, help him find another job that makes use of his people skills.

Yes, help him find another job.

Imagine the goodwill you'll earn from helping someone (who probably knows they're not suited for what they're doing) find a better fit. Imagine the goodwill you'll earn by helping one of your business peers find a naturally talented people pleaser to serve their customers.

If this seems difficult, risky, or just plain weird, go back and re-read the sections on Wolf's dilemma and cooperation. The option that brings the most benefit all around is often the one that feels risky. In the long run, though, these are the actions that define your company in the eyes of your employees, customers, and peers.

Managing People

Employees are people. Some companies don't realize that. They think employees are tools or equipment. Remember, with machines you can be efficient; with people, you have to be effective. This means a few changes from typical corporate mentality. Offices, for instance.

In a big corporation, offices declare how much you're paid. Programmers sit in cubicles in common areas. Executives, whether or not they need privacy, get offices.

I'm not suggesting executives shouldn't have offices, but folks who do any kind of mentally intensive problem-solving work, like programming or writing, need large blocks of uninterrupted time. And for these folks, 'uninterrupted' means zero interruptions, intentional or otherwise. It can take twenty or thirty minutes to get into the 'zone' where the code or prose or whatever is flowing, filling in the big picture instead of just being words or procedures. A single interruption, whether it's the person in the next cubicle asking for a phone number or a handful of folks talking as they leave for lunch, can cost this productive person another hour of getting their head back to that point again.

Don't assign office space, titles, or paychecks based on any preconceived notions about how it works in business today. Business today is essentially broken; don't perpetuate the flaws as you build your own little empire.

This is not Your Father's Management

A few decades ago, being a manager meant deciding what to do and how to do it, and getting others to act. It meant giving directions, usually quite specific, based on the rulebook, and expecting abject obedience. If you're managing like that, chances are your employees clip out Dilbert comics and write your name above the pointy-haired boss. It was never a very good idea. Today, it's fatal.

Your job as a manager now is very different. Since the folks on the front line, doing the actual work from day to day, really know what's going on, your job is basically to smooth their path. Get the right people in place, ensure they understand what you consider desirable outcomes, let them know why it's in their best interests to achieve them, and help them do so.

If you're mentoring the right people, who know what's expected and what's in it for them, you'll have a world-class team. If their striving, thinking and relating talents are suited to the outcomes you've defined, they'll find their own best way to succeed. They'll also feel special and important, not being treated like a cog in your wheel. Don't make them earn your trust; you hired them, remember? Give trust; distrust should be earned.

To do this you have to have a pretty clear vision of what you really want. You have to be able to convey to a delivery driver what you expect without trying to plan his route. The folks answering your phones won't need a script; they'll need a clear picture of how you want your callers to feel. Some outcomes are physical, like 'getting all packages to the people who ordered them, in good condition, just a little sooner than they expected them' and some are emotional, like 'they should feel important because we're really listening.'

Now, you don't have to decide if people are doing their jobs. Just look at the outcomes (meaning, measure them!) If the results are what you wanted, they're doing their jobs. Now you can get rid of the time clock, right? Who needs a time clock in a small company or department to know whether or not employees are doing their jobs? What this also means is moving away from paying people for their time, and toward paying them for their services. With engaged enthusiastic employees, the kind you'll have if you're doing it right, you'll get more from them than from folks who are working for a time clock.

Respect for the Individual

Since we've decided that employees are people, let's go a step further and assume they're individuals. Each one is different, and would like to be treated that way.

There is a direct relationship between how you treat people, your expectations, and how they react. Treat them like cogs and you'll get cogs. Treat them like responsible adults, and that's what you'll have. As long as your business goals have been clearly conveyed, these talented adults will find the best way to reach them.

This eliminates two common problems: defensive feelings about change, and destructive competition.

You're going to be measuring, collecting data all the time. If your employees are secure, knowing that you consider them talented adults, they won't worry that all this measuring is to find a way to cut out their jobs.

They'll also be able to benefit from the positive effects of competition. We're all competitive; some of us like to compete with others, some of us are driven to compete with ourselves. But when the competition is tied to a reward system (financial or recognition) it gets ugly really fast.

Most folks don't need to be paid to compete. Paying them is what corrupts it. Instead, make everyone's numbers (whatever you use for a measuring stick) public—in an absolutely non-judgmental way. Make it known from day one that everyone's production gets posted. Don't discuss it or reward it. Just make sure everyone knows how well they're doing. They'll compare themselves to whatever is their greatest driving factor: the person they work with closely, the top performer, themselves. And they'll do it because that's how we are, not because they're earning something with it.

Responsibility and Authority

One fundamental tenet of business management is that responsibility and authority should be equal; that is, if I'm responsible for something, I should have authority to ensure that it happens. If I have authority over something, I should be responsible for the outcome.

To see what happens when this isn't the case, watch the scene in "Joe Versus the Volcano" where Tom Hanks and Dan Hedaya discuss the advertising library, which is low on catalogs. Joe, responsible for the stock, isn't allowed to place orders with the printer. Hedaya's character, Mr. Waturi, one of the great Dilbertian characters of modern cinema, says, "I want those catalogs!" to which Joe replies, "Well, then, please order them."

Are your employees held responsible for customer satisfaction, without knowing they have the authority to create it? If a discount, freebie, refund, whatever, is what it would take right now to make this customer happy, either your employee has the authority to make it happen, or the customer had better have a way to contact you directly, right now, so someone with authority can take responsibility.

Do you have middle managers (or worse, upper management) who have authority to make demands, set deadlines, or create projects, but who then aren't held responsible? Sure, the CIO or Director of IT can set standards for response to help desk requests, but they'd better be ready to pony up the resources necessary to make it happen. It's all too common in the information technology world to assume that (and I quote an ex-employer here) "if you just work faster, you can get more done in less time." (No, I'm not kidding.)

Every time a manager, at any level, assigns responsibility to a direct report or their staff, they must either assign matching authority, or simply assign tasks, projects, or deliverables and retain responsibility for the end result themselves. Anything else is Machiavellian (in the pejorative sense.)

Subcontracting

Your business does not need to be limited to what you can do alone. It is fairly easy to find partners in the industry to work with you for services you don't specialize in. You can then subcontract the work to another virtual assistant.

Consult with your attorney or tax accountant to find out about any local laws or tax issues in your area that may apply.

When you subcontract, your reputation is still on the line. Interview potential subcontractors and make sure they will be a good fit for you and your clients.

In just the last couple of months I've been able to put together a team that can handle a variety of tasks when I need extra help. My three team members have done internet research, compiled contact databases, made telephone calls, and created and mailed out documents.

Managing Money

I'll repeat it here: profit is to a business what being healthy is to your body: you need it, you want as much as possible, but it's not the purpose, it's part of the process.

The short course on money management is to find a CFO for hire and have a talented tax accountant and advisor. I'm not going to pretend to give you an exhaustive treatise on how to manage money. Instead, just a few tips and warnings.

Pay Attention

Knowing what's going on is the best money management advice I can think of. A clear overall picture of everything having to do with your company's finances, updated regularly, will help avoid virtually all the pitfalls common to small business.

You should always see your bank and credit card statements. Limit the amount of money anyone else can spend (in cash or the company checking or charge account.) Over that amount, require a second signature, preferably your own. Make sure you never have a fox guarding the henhouse. Folks who order supplies should never be the ones who receive it. Folks who are authorized to pay for things shouldn't be authorized to order them without a second set of eyes involved.

If you're spending more money than you'd give as a gift, get everything in writing. Having everything clarified enough to be written down helps prevent confusion later. A contract, even a simple one, will also tell you exactly what you got for your money, and what you didn't. It can also act as a reminder when you paid for something and never got it.

Keep a tickler file for things awaiting delivery so you can follow up if things don't arrive. That includes services, too. One client paid for some web services, then didn't use them for a couple years. (If you're not ready to use something, don't buy it unless there's an overwhelming benefit to you.) When the client was ready to use the service, they couldn't remember exactly what they'd paid for, and the company had changed hands so it was a circus trying to get details from the new owners. Keep your own records and avoid that.

I used to work for a telecom consulting company. One of our processes was to compare invoices with the actual services received. It astonished me how common it was for billing to continue long after services had been turned off. In larger corporations, the process for approval and payment of these invoices is so full of holes that we often found tens of thousands of dollars worth of services being billed long after they were turned off.

Keep your personal and business finances separate. Put business money in a business account, and pay yourself either by a real wage or by making draws on the business account. It's not just a good accounting practice, but it helps set the right mental tone for yourself.

Most entrepreneurs can't afford a full-time accountant, but no entrepreneur can afford to be completely without an accountant. Get an accountant to review your financial practices. Hire a virtual office administrator who understands generally accepted accounting practices (and then, of course, have the systems they put in place reviewed by the professional accountant you're going to consult, right?)

Keeping Honest People Honest

We all like to assume that the people around us are honest. Your family, friends, employees wouldn't steal from you, right? The September 2007 issue of Entrepreneur magazine has an article entitled 'To Catch a Thief' which refers to a report from the Association of Certified Fraud Examiners regarding embezzlement losses during 2006. The ACFE's PowerPoint presentation of the report says "Small businesses continue to suffer disproportionate fraud losses. The median loss suffered by organizations with fewer than 100 employees was $190,000 per scheme. This was higher than the median loss in even the largest organizations."

If someone really wants to steal from you, they will. (The article quotes CPA Gary Zeune: "And what's the best way to prevent somebody from stealing from you? Don't hire them in the first place.") But even honest folks can be tempted. Even honest folks make 'mistakes' (meaning errors in judgment, not errors in accounting.)

Besides good hiring practices, the best way to keep your honest employees honest is to ensure that temptation just doesn't come along. If it's easy to fool around with the company's money, eventually it's likely to happen. If you have good accounting practices in place, it becomes an actual effort to steal, rather than allowing an otherwise honest employee to rationalize 'borrowing' a little from the company, intending to pay it back, or padding an expense account with something that wouldn't pass any real scrutiny.

When 'accounting' is the guy/gal across the office from you, the 'warehouse' is the closet, and 'reception' is whoever is answering the phone today, you're way, way better off preventing theft/fraud/stupidity than reacting to it. Even honest people can be tempted. It doesn't make them criminals; it's just an opportunity for a momentary act of stupidity.

Yes, you can catch jerks by leaving cash lying around and then checking hands for exploding orange dye. But if you catch otherwise good people in the same net for making a stupid judgment call they wouldn't otherwise even consider, are you better off as a businessperson, or more importantly, as a person, period?

Financial Matters

In order to make good business decisions, you need to have a basic understanding of financial matters. Do you understand what your profit and loss statement tells you? What percentage of your time is spent on administrative work versus billable client work?

"By modeling my cash flow and keeping a weekly eye on it I have managed to stay afloat, in credit and keep all suppliers bills paid. I think it is really key to any business to know the amount of cash available in the business and to model what will happen if any invoices are delayed. Tied in with this is credit control and how to make sure you are paid on time if you offer credit terms."
—Hannah Lewis, Fish in Custard, Small Business Assistance

Determining Your Rates

"I see so many VAs struggling because they undervalue their costs AND rates."
—Cynthia Papia, Office To-Go

"With the competition from other countries providing the same services for less, it is sometimes tempting to charge less just to get the client."
—Margie Gibson, MG Virtual Office Solutions

Setting your rates is an area that many virtual assistants find challenging. You may be tempted to charge less than you should just so you can get clients. However you need to remember that you are a business owner and you have costs that need to be covered. You'll also find that your services are taken more seriously when you charge appropriately.

Sue's Experience

One of my first clients told me that if I had told him I only charged $15 an hour, he would have found someone else. He expected to pay at least $25 per hour and thought I should charge even more than that. He said that if I didn't think my services were worth $25 an hour, why should he value my services?

Since my original conversation with this client a little over a year ago, I have raised my rates considerably on two different occasions. At the time I had five on my client list and now have 22 on my list. You do the math.

An experienced VA shares some very good information to help you determine your rates:

"The worst mistake I made in my business when I started out was 'rounding down' my bills, giving away time for free. My most important piece of advice for VAs is to charge for all your time! The Industry Production Standards (IPS Guide, Office Business Center Association Int'l, (their web address is http://www.obcai.org/index2.cfm?section=products) *is invaluable in helping you figure out how to do this and explain it to your clients. It's similar to the "blue book" that printers and mechanics use in estimating. Using the blue book may allow you to bill—in complete fairness to your client—for more than your actual time, rather than penalize yourself for your efficiency. If you charge $40/hr. and give away 5 minutes of every hour (5 hrs./day x 240 working days) you lose almost $5,000/year!*

Don't assume you have to 'shave off time' even if you're doing something you've never done. For instance, you might find yourself using an advanced feature of a program that is new to you and be tempted not to charge for your time, thinking if the client went to someone else they wouldn't have to pay for a learning curve. But because things in the computer field change so fast, chances are most other VAs don't know the program any better than you do. Be fair to yourself. If the technology is new, or you're one of the early adopters, your client is reaping the benefits of your new acquisition and should expect to pay for that advantage.

Another problem is charging too low an hourly rate. The tendency to underestimate charges is one of the main reasons people go out of business and have to return to the full-time working world. The biggest misconception is, "If I don't have the lowest rates around, people will go elsewhere." To the contrary; I found that once I raised my rates, I added credibility to myself as a professional.

When you set your rates too low, you often end up with the people who haggle over every nickel, and those are often the most difficult to work with.

Your hourly rate should also cover the costs of:

- *medical, disability, unemployment and theft insurance, retirement pension.*
- *sick leave (including the 9 paid holidays + 2 weeks vacation most employers provide)*
- *supplies*
- *advertising (including website, brochures/literature to send prospective, postage)*
- *the amount you to purchase equipment/software and fix and/or upgrade them*
- *self-employment, federal, state taxes*
- *cost of living increases. (The Consumer Price Index has gone up over 200% since I went into business in 1981, meaning that the $15 an hour I charged as a beginner translates to almost $35 an hour now, without even raising rates to reflect increased experience and efficiency.*

If you don't add these expenses and unpaid time to your hourly wage (often 50-75% of your total billing rate), you will be making significantly less than someone working for an employer. Do you want your own (or your family's) earnings to subsidize your clients' expenses? When clients try to get you to compromise on your rate, that's what they're asking you to do! Remember: the buck stops with you, so cover your costs, or you may have to go back to calling someone else 'boss'."

— Nina Feldman, Nina Feldman Connections

Chapter Seven: Customer Service

Nearly everything I have to say about customer service is covered in the sections on how people think. This section will focus on actual customer interaction; the stuff most of us think of when we think of customer service.

What Do You Expect?

I've rattled on endlessly about treating your customers like grown-ups, like special honored guests. Here's the other side of that coin: they're not the professionals; you are.

Don't expect your clientele to understand the technical jargon common to your industry. If I mention 'hosting', 'IP address', or 'domain name' to most of my clients, I get blank stares. That's okay; if they didn't need technical assistance I'd be out of work.

Stop and think about the terminology that's specific to your industry. If you're not absolutely positive your gramma (or better still, your neighbor's gramma) would understand it, find a simpler way to say it. It's fine to educate your customers, but don't expect them to educate themselves just to do business with you. Remember, making people feel dumb is not going to earn their business. Make them comfortable. That means not making them ask you what you're talking about.

Close to You

It's common for the owner of the company to become less accessible as it grows. For you, that's a good thing, because you get to focus on what you're best at, letting others handle what they're best at.

But don't make the mistake of making your customers talk to the busboy if you're the one grilling their steak (or veggie kabob, if that's your preference.)

It's common corporate thinking to have 'customer service' folks answering all the phones. You may have an administrative type or assistant managing customer interaction. If they've read this book and really care about people, you're probably in good shape. But don't isolate the customers from the people who are actually working on their solutions.

This is another way to differentiate yourself. Most companies make sure their technicians aren't bothered by customers. It's partly to keep the talent working, and partly because the talent often has minimal social skills. Make sure your talent (including you) knows that these customers allow us the privilege of being in business. Teach them whatever they need to excel at customer interaction. Now your clientele feels privileged because they get a glimpse into the inner workings of your company—and, just a little bit, it becomes their company.

This also makes responding to customers faster. Instead of waiting on hold for a customer service queue, you have a whole company full of folks who can help with most things. Even if it takes a call back from the *right* person, getting some kind of response from a real human, right away, makes all the difference in the world.

Earning Tips

No, not tips on earning. Learning to think in the moment, getting instant feedback on how you're doing.

Imagine if the only way your company made money was tips, based entirely on the quality of your customer service, not your product. The servers in your favorite restaurant don't have to imagine. The bulk of their income has nothing to do with the food they carried to the table.

This is a huge customer service advantage. Imagine if, after every single transaction, the customer told you in simple black and white terms how they felt about your service? Bellhops, skycaps and waiters know. They get a tip or they don't. If they do, it's big or it's not. If they're smart, they'll do more of what earns big tips, and less of what got none.

Every single customer interaction, you should know whether you've earned a tip, and how big it would be.

Ask. Yes, talk to your customers some more. And don't wait to mail some questionnaire through the mail or for them to take your online survey. If you can, ask before they pay your bill or hand their credit card to the cashier. If you can't do that, call (don't email) and ask them how you did. Ask them, point blank, if they'd recommend you to others. If not, find out what was broken and fix it. (Read up on the concept of Net Promoter Score and see how it can help you think like a waiter.)

Amazon.com Can't Live Without Me

Listening to the customer; responsibility and authority balance; so much of what I've talked about happens when I deal with Amazon.

Amazon lost my book. Okay, I'm pretty sure it was really the U.S. Postal Service. Their tracking software admits they picked it up from the warehouse a hundred miles from my house, but a month later it was still 'in transit' and USPS said they had no further information. They weren't unpleasant, they just didn't know.

Of course, the reason USPS has no real tracking information is because I cheaped out and accepted Amazon's free shipping instead of paying five bucks to have my $40 programming book delivered. (It's a business expense, fer cryin' out loud; pay for the shipping already.)

I finally got tired of waiting and emailed Amazon to ask how I submitted a claim for a lost book, or whether they'd even accept it since the postal service admitted they'd had the book. The email I received less than 24 hours later, from a company so huge they certainly won't die without my few shekels, said this, in part:

" . . . *one of the benefits we'd like to offer our customers is convenience, and I realize that we have not met that standard in this case. I hope that you will give us another opportunity to prove the quality of our service to you in the future."*

They shipped a new copy of the book, upgrading the shipping so it's traceable. Sure, they don't need my money. And it's highly unlikely most people would refuse to do business with Amazon just because you had to hit up the USPS for lost mail.

But this isn't about a few dollars for one book. Amazon went so far beyond what I expected that even if I have another unpleasant experience, I'll still be a raving fan. A raving fan who tells others about the surprisingly great customer service I got.

When your customer needs service, don't make them worry about whose fault it was, or how this is going to get fixed. Just fix it. Surprise them with excellence, and the few bucks it'll cost you will be one of the best marketing investments you make this year.

For even more love stories, search for 'Zappos shoes' on the internet. It's pretty impressive.

Everyone is not Equal

Here's another concept I don't understand: special pricing for new customers.

Why on earth would you punish or insult your existing loyal customers by making them pay more than someone who just walked through the door?

Treat your loyal customers like royalty. (Make up a little rhyme about 'loyal' and 'royal' if you like.) Make it clear to them that you know you wouldn't be in business if it weren't for them.

There are other ways to attract new business. Focusing on money sends the wrong message to prospects and suspects.

What Do They Want? (Redux)

You cannot guess what your customers want. You know the danger of assuming. If you don't know what your clientele values you can't provide it.

We all tend to assume that everyone thinks like we do. We're all wrong. If you assume that the customers whose cars you repair are concerned about getting them back quickly, but what they really care about is getting them back clean, you could make a poor impression without realizing it.

Practical Efficiency as it Effects Customers

You've probably read the sign on the wall of a local business that says "Fast. Cheap. Top Quality. Pick two."

Of course, your customers want all three. If you can provide all three, you just set yourself apart from the folks who hung that sign. Here are a few tips from the concepts of six sigma thinking which can help to some extent. For even more information, you could read Michael George's "Lean Six Sigma for Service" or you can contact me for a down-to-earth version of the whole concept.

They're Always On Your Mind

Considering the customer in every phase of your work can be the most effective streamlining tool you've got. Every step of every task you perform either adds value in the customer's eyes, or it doesn't. Your job is to eliminate the non-value tasks, as far as possible. According to Michael George, work that adds no value in the customer's eyes typically makes up 50% of the cost in a service business. This leaves plenty of room for improvement.

Not all non-value-added steps can be eliminated. Most accounting processes add little in the customer's eyes, but they're necessary. Filing necessary government-mandated paperwork does nothing to benefit your clients directly, but can't be ignored.

But consider some other processes and methods. Do you batch similar work together, doing it all on the same day each week or month, or at the same time each day? Ponder your process and consider: is this really the best service to your customer, or is it for your own convenience? Of course, if the two align, that's great. If not, serve your customer, not yourself.

I used to ask my web clients to email me information for their websites. It's obviously easier and more accurate to copy and paste information they've already typed than to transcribe it from paper or a phone call.

Easier, that is, for me, not them.

Now, we let clients know they can use any communication method they like. If it makes them feel cared for to call us on the phone and chat a bit while we take notes on what they really seem to want, that's what we do. In the end, it really is easier and more accurate to do it this way because they're doing what's comfortable and familiar, allowing them to focus on the end result, not the process. Process is our job.

As you go through your day, imagine the customer watching over your shoulder. Would they feel they were getting good value for their money, or would they be saying "Why are we wasting time on *this*?" Come up with a good answer, or come up with a different process.

Are You Sure That's What They Want?

I hope I've mentioned it enough: don't guess what your customers want. Find out. Know for sure.

A graph comparing how important a benefit is to your customers with their perception of your delivery can be very revealing. Using a scale that allows for easy comparison, create a bar chart showing the relative importance of each benefit customers expect. Overlay a line chart of their perception of how well you deliver that benefit. If the delivery line skims the tops of each benefit bar, you're focusing on what's important to your customers. But where the line dips into the bar, customers think you're not delivering.

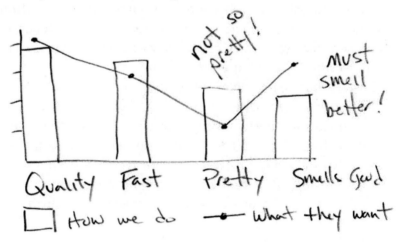

Keep it simple, though. Customers are doing you a favor to answer questions and take surveys. Make sure they know you appreciate it. Be careful not to abuse their time for your benefit. A handful of questions about a handful of concepts is enough for a bite-sized baby-step toward a little bit of excellence.

Further Resources

We feel like we've left so much out. Despite that, quite a bit made it in.

In Chapter One, "How We Think" we talked about all the psychological stuff that applies to yourself, customers, employees, vendors and competitors.

That laid the groundwork, showing the value of the next chapter on "Personal Development." We included the personal habits of ethics, punctuality and cleanliness, and talked about dress. We spent some time on important social skills for business. That included your speech, writing email, and using the phone.

All this contributes to the goal of Chapter Three, "Getting Things Done." I hope it's clear now why reading and writing (well, and often) are critical business skills. I hope you're not afraid of a little business math, and appreciate some of the dangers of innumeracy. This chapter included some thoughts on efficiency and project management.

All this stuff should help you develop good business strategy, the topic of Chapters Four and Five. Chapter Four covered marketing; both your current products or services and developing new stuff. Along with Chapter Five, covering the rest of business strategy, it's the practical application of "How We Think " and sees practical application itself in "Business Operations" in Chapter Six.

Chapter Six went over staffing, managing people and managing money, leading to the ultimate goal of the book, "Customer Service" in Chapter Seven. This final chapter, combined with all the chapters leading up to it will help you create an excellent customer experience. It's the purpose of this book. It should be the purpose of your business, because that's the key to it all.

So, where do we go from here?

A few suggestions:

· The reading list includes virtually all the books which have filled my head with the seeds which became this book. I've rated them for readability, not value. Their value depends on your needs at any particular time. But if you know one book is a quick read and the other is a weighty tome, maybe it'll help you choose the one that's right for right now.

· Email us. Tell us what you liked; what inspired you. Tell us where we're way off base. Tell us what helped you. Ask questions. Remind us of all those places where we said "I'll come back to that later" and never did. Make suggestions about the next edition of this book. It'll be published in small handcrafted batches like a really good beer, so your thoughts may very well end up in the next edition (and your name in the acknowledgments, should you so desire.)

· Hire Joel. Yes, despite his huge success as an author, he still loves public speaking, training, and face-to-face one-on-one sessions with people like us who are trying to make a living doing what they love, and just need a little nudge in the right direction now and then.

Of course, if you read voraciously, putting into practice what makes sense to you from the minds, mouths and pens of the thinkers of the new millennium, you'll never need to hire someone to help you succeed. You'll be setting the standard for others to follow. H'ray, you!

In Conclusion

(I wanted to give Sue the last word. She wanted to give some of her professional associates the last word. Sue won.)
I wholeheartedly agree with Rachel, who says:

"I love my work. In fact, there are so many things to rave about that I wouldn't know where to begin. I love partnering with my clients to grow their business, I love the variety of projects I get to tackle, I love delving into new and exciting industries, I love to hear "How did I ever manage without you?!"
—Rachel Rasmussen, Rescue Desk, LLC

"Living on a farm in Wisconsin, I never thought there would be chance to supplement my income and do it while at home. Having two small kids and working full-time there was no way for me to have a second job outside the home.

I live in a rural area and jobs are quite scarce if WAH didn't work out. So, starting slow has helped. I switched jobs and less stress gave me more time to really do some calling for opportunities. Then I met my mentor, Diane Hess, Certified Virtual Professional Coach. Until I was given the opportunity to have hands on experience with Diane Hess, I really didn't feel like I had much to offer.

Now, limiting my availability and making sure I stay fair to the family is my biggest hurdle. In a few years if I can pay for a family trip to Disney World, that will be my final decision-maker to do this full-time."

—Collette Schultz , Virtual Dream Office Services
http://virtualdreamofficeservices.blogspot.com/

From the Trenches: Tips and Tricks from Successful VAs

Sue's Thoughts On Competition

It's my goal to create an atmosphere of sharing within the VA industry of knowledge and resources. We can each help one another out. There's no need to keep secret what it takes to succeed. If you're a successful VA, reach out to someone who is just getting started and offer to be a mentor. I was just contacted by an aspiring VA in Washington and Joel and I have agreed to a half-hour phone consultation each week to mentor and coach her so she too can become a successful virtual assistant. It's an exciting place to be!

We asked virtual assistants "What does a VA need to know to succeed in business?" Throughout the book we've included some of their comments and suggestions and this section contains even more.

These VAs have given us permission to share their tips and tricks with you. Feel free to contact any of them and they will be happy to share what they know with you.

What does a VA need to know to succeed in business?

- *Research what you're going to name your business, put a lot of thought into this as this will stay with you forever.*
- *Research domain names and don't be too quick to get one.*
- *When purchasing a domain name, purchase for more than one year, this shows longevity and credibility.*
- *Take classes to heighten and sharpen skills or to learn something new.*
- *Obtain certifications if necessary for tasks you will be performing.*
- *Research what sort of website you want, blog, Wordpress, etc.*
- *What sort of licenses is required in your state or county?*
- *Research liability insurance for your particular niche and business.*
- *What do I have to offer? What have I done in the past or currently doing that I absolutely love doing? Find what your niche is.*
- *How are my skills better or different than others? Why would someone choose my services over others?*
- *How do I market my business?*

- *Research other VA rates and see how you fit into that category and are qualified to charge that particular amount.*
- *Learn the basics of HTML, SEO, blogging, article marketing if you don't already have this skill set.*
- *Make sure your typing, spelling and grammar skills are all up to speed.*
- *Learn how to prioritize and organize.*
- *Join networking sites related to your business and services and share ideas, be active within the community of these particular sites.*
- *You must have a positive attitude, be able to work independently and flexibility.*

—Deb Lamb, Your Everything Services
A Virtual Assistant Services Company
877-500-2793 toll free
www.youreverythingservices.com
youreverythingservices@gmail.com

More Advice from Successful VAs

"One component I'd suggest is that being a VA often means being a good forward-thinker. A one-time project that might not bring in much short-term income may turn into a long-term relationship; good for more projects. It's easy to turn down work that might not be solid from the start.

If I do not know how to do something, I say that and am up-front with clients regarding my skill-level. However, I have spent a lot of time researching for clients I knew I wasn't going to contract with realizing that this was an opportunity to increase my skill level and offer the jobs to other VAs more capable than myself. In other words, never just say, "I can't do this" rather, say, "I can't do this but I can offer this information and so-so can assist you with the project." People appreciate when their needs are just not dropped and that effort is shown to help them out. This may lead to a future client.

I've learned that the job can be lonely even if you have children, pets or seniors to care for while working from home. It's important to recognize that if a VA feels isolated (as I had) that there are ways to combat this situation and act upon it with support, exercise, good diet, et al.

Right now I'm struggling with technology moving faster than I can keep up. I feel overwhelmed with lists of 'things' I want to learn to improve my services and I struggle with chopping down that list to bite-sized-pieces I can digest. Lately, my days are working, learning and marketing with some days where the learning takes over a good portion of the day. "

—**Jan, Your Virtual Wizard**

"The biggest challenges when I launched my business was having to constantly explain the term "virtual assistant" and having people state that my rate was too high.

Fast forward two years and I'm pleased to say that I no longer have to explain what a virtual assistant is and have a growing roster of ideal clients - aka - clients who understand and have experienced first-hand the value and benefits of working with me and willingly pay my fee.

I also graduated from a virtual assistance training program, as well as an Entrepreneurial Assistance Program offered by the local Chamber of Commerce. I firmly believe those two actions gave me the knowledge and self-confidence to stand firm when questioned on pricing.

Maintaining a high degree of professionalism and integrity and not reducing rates is critical to our success as business owners and to the virtual assistance industry as a whole. "

—**Rosalind Harris, CPS®**

"I think it's vital that virtual assistants - both rookies and veterans -- incorporate business-focused professional development in their plans."
—Rachel Rasmussen, Rescue Desk, LLC

Acknowledgments

We would like to thank all the virtual assistants who contributed their thoughts, ideas, suggestions, tips and tricks. Sue would especially like to thank:

- Leigh Anne Aston, Aston Administrative Services (http://www.astonadminservices.com)
- Nina Feldman, Nina Feldman Connections (http://www.NinaFeldman.com)
- Kelly Harris, Founder of FindVirtual.com (http://www.FindVirtual.com)
- Deb Lamb, Your Everything Services (http://www.youreverythingservices.com)
- Rachel Rasmussen, Rescue Desk, LLC (http://www.rescuedeskva.com)
- Collette Schultz, Virtual Dream Office Services (http://virtualdreamofficeservices.blogspot.com)

Thank you all!

- Jennifer Dillon, Collaborative Connections (http://www.ccvirtually.com)
- Lee Drozak, My Office Assistant (http://www.MyOfficeAssist.org)
- Beth Eckert, Virtual Office Express (http://www.VirtualOfficeExpress.com)

- Margie Gibson, MG Virtual Office Solutions (http://mgvirtualofficesolutions.org)
- Cindy Greenway, Hot Skills VA Training (http://www.hotskillsvatraining.com)
- Janine Gregor, YourVirtualWizard.com (http://www.YourVirtualWizard.com)
- Rosalind Harris, CPS®, Instant Assistant (http://www.instantassistant.net)
- Hannah Lewis, Fish in Custard, Small Business Assistance (http://www.fishincustard.com.co.uk)
- Heike Miller, PA Excellence Limited (http://www.heikemiller.com)
- Jessica Nix, Virtually Linked (http://www.virtuallylinkedva.com)
- Cynthia Papia, Office To-Go (http://www.officeto-go.com)
- Michele Randolph, Gold Force Administrative Support (http://www.goldforcesupport.com)
- Vickie Turley, A Balanced Alternative (http://www.abalancedalternative.com)

Recommended Websites

The web changes faster than I can type, but these websites have been around a while so the addresses should still be good. The latest version is available at my website, and as always, Google is your friend.

Our website (http://BizBa6.com) has links to resources, an ongoing reading list, and continuous new content.

FindVirtual.com (http://www.FindVirtual.com) is a social network for virtual assistants. This is a great resource to find information about the VA industry, ask questions, and grow your network.

Another social networking site, Virtual Assistant Forums (http://www.VirtualAssistantForums.com) is a discussion forum for virtual assistants at all levels of business development.

LinkedIn.com (http://www.LinkedIn.com) has two virtual assistant groups you can join and where you can post questions. They are the VA Industry Group and the Virtual Assistant Group. You can find Sue's profile at http://www.linkedin.com/in/suecanfield and Joel's at http://www.linkedin.com/in/joeldcanfield.

Seth Godin's weblog (http://SethGodin.typepad.com) is the most widely read business blog. It's updated almost every day and contains some of the most insightful observations on marketing and business you're going to find. Trying to create a marketing plan without reading Seth's work is silly. Don't do it.

Tom Peters and his team update his weblog (http://www.TomPeters.com) at least daily. The conversations in the comments section are lively and mentally stimulating. I've met some fine people in the brouhaha that ensues.

One of those fine people is Trevor Gay, author and consultant to the U.K.'s National Health who thinks an awful lot like I do. This means, among other things, a fairly unusual sense of humour. His weblog (http://www.SimplicityITK.blogspot.com) focuses on his passion for simplicity in business.

The Brand Autopsy weblog, administered by John Moore (http://BrandAutopsy.typepad.com) is always an interesting companion to Seth and Tom Peters. Sometimes John falls right in line, and sometimes he falls right between. Always fun, always educational.

The Personal MBA (http://PersonalMBA.com) is the brilliant idea of Josh Kaufman. Based on the concept that intelligent adults are capable of teaching themselves, he calls it 'do-it-yourself business education.' The website is home to a frequently updated reading list of what Josh considers the truly essential business knowledge, in a self-teaching format. It's my Amazon.com wish list source.

The online home of solid, free software is 37 Signals (http://www.37signals.com), the home of Basecamp, Highrise, Backpack, and Campfire, free online organizational and collaboration tools.

SCORE (http://www.score.org) is an organization of business professionals and educators which provides free mentoring and education to entrepreneurs. Their goal is to promote the formation, growth and success of small businesses. Although it's no substitute for a live mentor nearby, these folks are genuinely interested in helping.

The Small Business Association (http://www.sba.gov) has boatloads of helpful information both in print and at their website. More free resources.

Your local Small Business Development Center can be found at the SBA's website (the enormous long link is below.) The SBDC is another fantastic free resource. Business professionals in your own area will meet with you on a regular basis to help with your business plan, marketing, and overall reality check. The sense of accountability is worth the effort of making an appointment. (http://www.sba.gov/aboutsba/sbaprograms/sbdc/sbdclocat or/SBDC_LOCATOR.html)

Rummage around at the One Page Business Plan© website (http://www.onepagebusinessplan.com) for all you'll need to create your own simple, straightforward business plan.

Recommended Reading List

The rating on each book is readability, not value. The letters are F for 'fun to read' and D for 'deep material.' The numbers are a general indication of long (3), short (2), or really short (1).

- Buckingham, Marcus and Coffman, Curt. *First, Break All the Rules: What the World's Greatest Managers Do Differently.* Simon & Schuster, 1999. A real eye-opening read about front line management. They spend quite a bit of time on the concepts of skills, knowledge, and talent, discussing their role in hiring and management. Not just for managers, though; anyone who wants to be a stellar employee or happy entrepreneur can benefit from the same concepts. *(F2)*
- Carnegie, Dale. *How to Win Friends and Influence People.* Pocket, 1998. If you only own one book on dealing with human relationships this should be it. I read it once a year and get something new every time. Clear and simple tools to help you present yourself to others in the best light, and to understand how people think. Just plain good advice for business, marriage, or life. *(F2)*
- George, Michael L. *Lean Six Sigma for Service: How to Use Lean Speed and Six Sigma Quality to Improve Services and Transactions.* McGraw–Hill, 2003. A weighty tome applying the Lean and Six Sigma manufacturing concepts to service businesses. It's a difficult read, not just because of the technical jargon and statistical bent, but in many places it could have

benefited from a good editor. If you can wade through the verbiage, though, the concepts are priceless. If you're serious about streamlining processes and really fine-tuning your service business, this book could really help. *(D3)*

- *Getting Real.* 37signals, LLC, 2006. You can buy the dead tree version, or download the PDF free from their website. It's really about writing software, but many of the concepts apply to management and marketing in any business. *(F2)*
- Godin, Seth. *All Marketers are Liars: The Power of Telling Authentic Stories in a Low Trust World.* Portfolio Hardcover, 2005. Don't let the title fool you; it's about telling the truth, not lying. Storytelling is the best marketing. This book explains the concepts and gives concrete examples with Seth's usual wit and precision. *(F2)*
- Godin, Seth. *The Bootstrapper's Bible: How to Start and Build a Business With a Great Idea and (Almost) No Money.* Upstart Pub Co, 1998. Available from Amazon as a PDF download. No one should start a new business without reading this. Much here to help even existing small businesses. *(F1)*
- Godin, Seth. *The Dip: A Little Book That Teaches You When to Quit (and When to Stick) .* Portfolio Hardcover, 2007. This book doesn't give you the answers, it asks you the questions. Without 'The Dip' I probably wouldn't have pursued a career as a speaker and writer, and might not be recording my own music. Knowing when to quit is useful. Knowing when not to quit is better. *(F1)*
- Godin, Seth. *Free Prize Inside: The Next Big Marketing Idea.* Portfolio Hardcover, 2004. I had a lot of fun reading this. It sparks thoughts like a one-man brainstorming session. As with all of Seth's books,

read it once as an overview, then again to take notes. *(F2)*

- Godin, Seth. *Permission Marketing: Turning Strangers Into Friends And Friends Into Customers.* Simon & Schuster, 1999. You cannot create a meaningful marketing plan without this book. *(F2)*
- Godin, Seth. *Purple Cow: Transform Your Business by Being Remarkable.* Portfolio Hardcover, 2004. Remarkable can me amazing, and it can mean 'worth talking about.' This teaches concepts that help with both. *(F2)*
- Godin, Seth. *Survival Is Not Enough: Zooming, Evolution and the Future of Your Company.* Simon & Schuster, 2002. Seth's only weighty tome, it uses evolution as an analogy for embracing change in business. The analogy isn't perfect and the book is long. Plenty of useful information, worth digging out. *(D3)*
- Godin, Seth. *Unleashing the Ideavirus.* Hyperion, 2001. The granddaddy of them all, this explains how to make your product or service create its own word-of-mouth marketing. *(F2)*
- Molloy, John T. *Dress for Success.* Grand Central Publishing, 1988. Stuck in the 70s, the examples aren't always relevant, but the concepts can help you analyze your appearance. More about awareness than practical solutions, but worth reading. *(F2)*
- Paulos, John Allen. *Innumeracy: Mathematical Illiteracy and Its Consequences.* Hill and Wang, 2001. I love math, but even if you hate it, this is a fun book. He debunks myths, proves some common beliefs, and generally makes math and statistics and probability and chance seem fun. Like a self-defense class for the innumerate. *(F2)*

- Peters, Thomas J and Waterman Jr, Robert H. *In Search of Excellence: Lessons from America's Best-Run Companies.* Harpercollins, 1982. Long, deep, and complex, but well-written and packed with insights, anecdotes, and good reasoning. Don't be put off by the fact that many of the excellent companies profiled have slipped in the 25 since it was published. They were analyzed while still excellent, and the lessons are still valuable. *(D3)*
- Strunk Jr, William and White, E B. *The Elements of Style.* Allyn & Bacon, 1999. Priceless writing advice. Don't pick up a pen without it. *(F1)*
- Young, Pam and Jones, Peggy. *Sidetracked Home Executives.* Grand Central Publishing, 2001. Priceless organizing advice. Create your own personalized system for getting and staying organized. The sisters have the ability to laugh at themselves, but they took this challenge seriously. One of the great realizations was that most information on getting things done was created by people who were born organized. Young and Jones are like the rest of us; they had to work at it. It makes their advice infinitely more practical. *(F2)*
- Donald Norman. *The Design of Everyday Things*, Basic Books, 2002. Beautiful reasoning on why design is vital to meaningful life, and how bad design hurts. *(F3)*
- Roam, Dan. *The Back of the Napkin*, Portfolio Hardcover, 2008. Dan Roam believes that any problem can be solved by drawing a picture, and that anyone can draw it. (http://www.TheBackOfTheNapkin.com) *(F2)*
- Chip and Dan Heath. *Made to Stick*, Random House, 2007. The Heath brothers explain marketing through telling simple unexpected concrete credible emotional stories. (http://www.MadeToStick.com) *(F2)*

Index

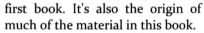

About Joel

Joel D Canfield is a web application developer turned business consultant. He's written two more business books, 49 Commonsense Business Observations, a 109-page introduction to his peculiar style of business thinking, and The Commonsense Entrepreneur, a fuller treatment of the subject of his

first book. It's also the origin of much of the material in this book.

Joel has successfully operated his own small businesses during the past 25 years and worked with and for service related small businesses for over 30 years. He has experience on the front line in customer service and service implementation, and in virtually all aspects of the back office: accounting, management, credit and collections, data entry, information technology, labor, design, and facilities/maintenance. In addition, he is a digital coach, helping people of all kinds to get the most from technology without becoming a slave to it.

As if that weren't enough, he is also, in no discernable order: a husband, father of seven, musician and songwriter, and a genuinely polite person. Oh, and he wants to live in the west of Ireland someday.

If you have comments or questions or would like to see how Joel can help your small business, he'd love to hear from you.

About Sue

Sue L Canfield's experience in Administrative Assistance began in 1994, working for a local office supply store. Since then she has worked in several different industries including the automotive, real estate, and Internet industries.

As General Manager of Joel's business since 2003, her  responsibilities include all accounting tasks, appointment setting, creating proposals, assisting with website design and creating web-based tools for small businesses.

As a virtual office administrator, her mission is to partner with her clients, helping them save time and money by providing administrative and marketing support. Working together they create and implement strategies to promote their businesses. Values of sincere interest, reliability, high integrity and remarkable service motivate clients to refer her services to others.

Her hobbies include poetry, reading, planning a move to Ireland someday, and spending time with friends and family.

Contact Information

Joel D & Sue L Canfield
286 Alta Vista Avenue
Roseville CA 95678
(877) 3 BIZBA6
Contact@BizBa6.com
http://BizBa6.com

CPSIA information can be obtained at www.ICGtesting.com
Printed in the USA
LVOW101924130212

268486LV00019B/131/P